GEOLOGY
OF THE
PACIFIC
NORTHWEST

INVESTIGATE HOW THE EARTH WAS FORMED

with **15** PROJECTS

CYNTHIA LIGHT BROWN
Illustrated by Eric Baker

Nomad Press
A division of Nomad Communications
10 9 8 7 6 5 4 3 2 1

This book was manufactured by Sheridan Books,
Ann Arbor, MI USA.
May 2011, Job # 325132
ISBN: 978-1-936313-39-6

Illustrations by Eric Baker

Questions regarding the ordering of this book should be addressed to
Independent Publishers Group
814 N. Franklin St.
Chicago, IL 60610
www.ipgbook.com

Nomad Press
2456 Christian St.
White River Junction, VT 05001
www.nomadpress.net

green press
INITIATIVE

~Titles in the *Build It Yourself* **Series~**

~CONTENTS~

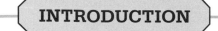
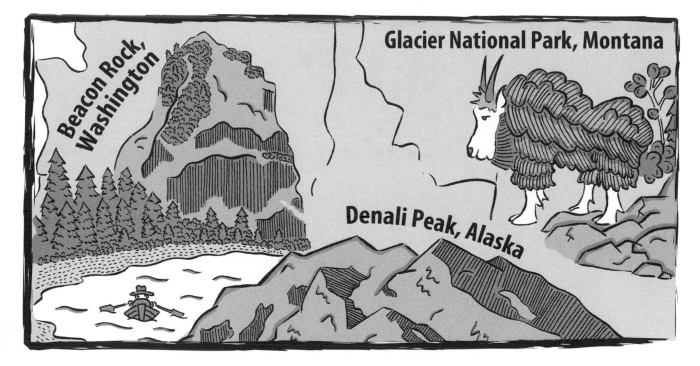

Beacon Rock, Washington

Glacier National Park, Montana

Denali Peak, Alaska

GEOLOGY & GEOGRAPHY

The Pacific Northwest is a land of exciting contrasts. It has the largest annual snowfall in the world. It has rainforests, and it has deserts. The Pacific Northwest also has some of our nation's greatest natural wonders, such as the mighty Columbia River, majestic Denali Peak, and rugged Glacier National Park.

How did these amazing landscapes form? Why are they so different from other parts of the country? Most of the Pacific Northwest wasn't even part of the original North American continent, but was stitched together like a patchwork quilt. That stitching is still going on, which causes explosive volcanoes and rumbling earthquakes.

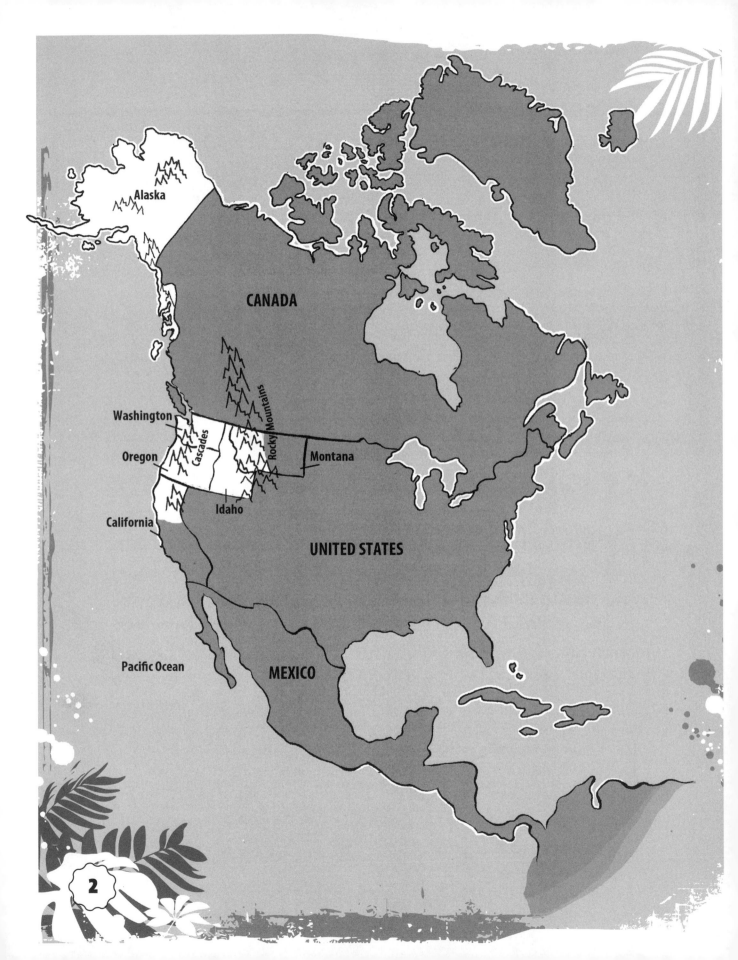

Alaska

CANADA

Washington

Cascades

Oregon

Rocky Mountains

Montana

Idaho

California

UNITED STATES

Pacific Ocean

MEXICO

In this book, you'll learn about the **geology** and physical **geography** of the Pacific Northwest. You'll read about the great forces that have shaped the region's mountains, rivers, weather, and **ecosystems**. You'll also come across some interesting trivia facts.

Did you know that the highest mountain in the United States is in the Pacific Northwest? And that the region holds the United States record for the largest temperature change in one day? As you read through this book, you'll get to work on a lot of exciting experiments and projects. They will help you understand the concepts better, like how fog forms on the West Coast.

WORDS TO KNOW

geology: the scientific study of the history and physical nature of the earth.

geography: the study of the earth and its features, especially the shape of the land, and the effect of human activity on the earth.

ecosystem: a community of plants and animals living in the same area and relying on each other to survive.

atmosphere: the air surrounding the earth.

hydrosphere: the earth's water, including oceans, rivers, lakes, glaciers, and water vapor in the air.

GEOLOGY: MORE THAN JUST ROCKS

Most people think of geology as the study of rocks. It certainly includes that, but it's much more. When you look at a rock, you can describe its color and shape. But what is even more interesting is how that rock formed and how it got to its present location. That involves seeing the big picture—the picture of the whole earth.

Geology is the scientific study of the history and physical nature of the earth. It explains how the color and shape of a rock gives clues to the history of that rock.

Geology involves the huge movements of the earth's crust. It also involves the systems of the **atmosphere** and **hydrosphere**, because air and water affect the breakdown and formation of rocks. And the geology of the Pacific Northwest tells an exciting part of that story.

GEOGRAPHY: MORE THAN JUST STATES AND CAPITALS

Just as geology is about more than just rocks, geography is about more than just states and their capitals. These are important, but geography tells a bigger story.

WORDS TO KNOW

climate: the average weather of an area over a long period of time.

There are two parts to geography. Physical geography includes things like mountains, rivers, **climate**, and the shape of the land. The second part of geography is how people interact with the land. This is called cultural geography and it includes things like population, agriculture, and recreation. An example of cultural geography would be how people affect the flow of a river by building dams or cities on it.

The geography of the Pacific Northwest includes a lot of sprawling mountain ranges. This makes the borders of the region hard to define. For example, the northern Rocky Mountains cover Idaho, but they also extend into western Montana. The Cascade Mountains run through the states of Washington and Oregon, but also into the very northern part of California.

This book covers all of the states of Washington, Oregon, Idaho, and Alaska, as well as western Montana and the northern section of California. It focuses on the geology and physical geography of the Pacific Northwest.

Are you ready to explore the thundering waterfalls, active volcanoes, and surging glaciers of the Pacific Northwest? Then let's go and visit this incredible land of and adventure!

CHAPTER 1

PLATE TECTONICS SHAPE
OUR LAND AND SEA

What is the driving force behind the formation of the different landscapes in the Pacific Northwest? You need to understand **plate tectonics**.

Plate tectonics is a scientific theory developed in the 1960s. It says that the outer layer of the earth is made up of interconnected plates that are constantly moving around. Volcanoes, mountains, valleys, and earthquakes all happen when and where they do because of the movement of the earth's plates. To understand plate tectonics, first let's look inside the earth.

WORDS TO KNOW

crust: the thin, brittle, outer layer of the earth. Together with the upper mantle, it forms the lithosphere.

brittle: describes a solid that breaks when put under pressure. A blade of grass will bend, but a dry twig is brittle and will break.

mantle: the middle layer of the earth. The upper mantle, together with the crust, forms the lithosphere.

lithosphere: the rigid outer layer of the earth that includes the crust and the upper mantle.

asthenosphere: the semi-molten middle layer of the earth that includes the lower mantle. Much of the asthenosphere flows slowly, like Silly Putty.

core: the center of the earth, composed of the metals iron and nickel. The core has two parts—a solid inner core, and a liquid outer core.

A PEEK INSIDE

The earth is made up of three main layers. They have different chemical compositions and physical properties.

The **crust** is the thin, outer layer of the earth. This is the layer that we walk on. It's solid but **brittle**, which means that it breaks when under pressure.

The **mantle** is the layer below the crust. It is hotter and denser here because the temperature and pressure inside the earth increase the deeper you go. The upper mantle is brittle and solid. Together, the crust and the upper mantle form the **lithosphere**, or the hard outer layer of the earth. The lithosphere is broken into plates. Below the plates is a layer called the **asthenosphere**. It is partially molten and can flow slowly without breaking—a bit like Silly Putty.

The **core** is the center of the earth. It is extremely dense and made up of iron and nickel. There's an inner core, which is solid because the pressure is so great, and an outer core, which is liquid. The core is almost as hot as the sun—about 9,000 degrees Fahrenheit (5,000 degrees Celsius)!

THE EARTH'S PUZZLE

The hard outer layer of the earth, the lithosphere, is broken up into about 12 large sections, called plates. There are also several smaller plates. The plates fit together like a jigsaw puzzle. Most of the plates are part **oceanic** and part **continental**. For example, the North American Plate includes nearly all of North America and the western half of the Atlantic Ocean.

WORDS TO KNOW

oceanic: in or from the ocean.

continental: relating to the earth's large land masses.

The plates are in constant slow motion! That's because the layer just under the plates—the asthenosphere—is very hot. The heat causes the molten rocks there to move around in huge rotating currents called convection cells. These convection cells move the plates above, which are floating like rafts on the hot goo below. The plates also help themselves move along. The older part of a plate is colder and denser. When it sinks into the mantle it pulls the rest of the plate with it and keeps the cycle going. Plates move somewhere between 1 to 6 inches per year (2½ to 15 centimeters).

Did You Know?

You might have heard of the earth's plates being sections of the earth's crust. That's partly correct. The tectonic plates are made of the crust and the upper mantle, which together are called the lithosphere. But most people just call it the crust because it's easier to remember.

ON THE EDGE

Volcanoes and earthquakes don't just happen anywhere. They're arranged in patterns. For example, there are lots of volcanoes around the rim of the Pacific Ocean, but there are none in Kansas. That's because most of the action happens where one plate meets another. This is called a plate boundary. There are three different kinds of plate boundaries.

Divergent plate boundaries are where two plates move apart from each other. They do this because the hot molten goo beneath, called **magma**, is pushing upward. This causes **rifting**. The hot goo pushes out and solidifies to form new rocks. Nearly all of the earth's new crust forms at divergent boundaries. An example of a divergent boundary is about 280 miles off the coast of Oregon and Washington (450 kilometers). Rifting is occurring there at the Juan de Fuca Ridge.

Convergent plate boundaries are where two plates collide. What happens depends on whether the plates are oceanic or continental.

One type of collision is when an oceanic plate collides with a continental plate. Because the oceanic plate is denser and thinner than the continental plate, it slides underneath the continental plate. This is called **subduction**.

As the subducted oceanic plate sinks lower, its weight pulls the rest of the plate along as well. The sinking plate encounters a lot of heat and pressure. This causes the plate to release hot gas and steam, which rises and melts the rock above. The melted rock, the magma, also rises to the surface, creating volcanoes. In the Pacific Northwest, this is happening right now to create the Cascade Mountains with explosive volcanoes like Mount St. Helens.

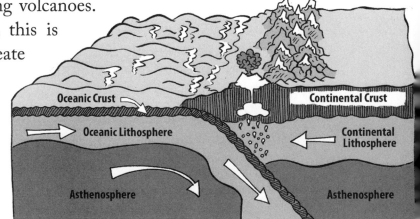

Oceanic Continental Convergance

Oceanic Crust
Continental Crust
Oceanic Lithosphere
Continental Lithosphere
Asthenosphere
Asthenosphere

If a continental plate collides with another continental plate, they both buckle upwards, forming mountains. That's what is happening now where the Indian Plate and the Eurasian Plate are colliding. The result is the Himalaya Mountains, which include the highest mountain in the world, Mt. Everest. Long ago, the Brooks Range in northern Alaska formed when continental crust slammed into North America.

WORDS TO KNOW

transform boundary: where two plates slide against each other.

hotspot: an area that can be found in the middle of a plate, where hot magma rises to the surface.

Transform plate boundaries are where two plates grind against each other as they move side by side in opposite directions. As the plates move past each other they sometimes suddenly slip. This creates a big lurch, or earthquake. The famous San Andreas Fault in California is part of a transform boundary between the North American and Pacific Plates. This is why California has so many earthquakes. A transform boundary also runs through Denali National Park in Alaska.

Hotspots are areas of strong geologic activity, but they aren't on the edge of plates. Hotspots are small, extremely hot regions that usually occur in the middle of a plate. They exist because hot material, probably from deep in the mantle, makes its way to the surface. The Hawaiian Islands formed when the Pacific Plate slowly made its way over a hotspot. There's also a hotspot that is now beneath Yellowstone National Park, located where Wyoming, Idaho, and Montana meet.

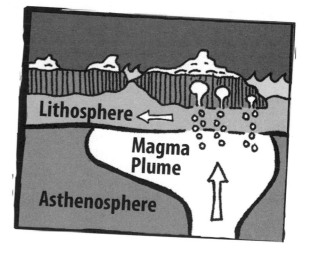

GIANT CONVEYOR BELT

The movement of the plates acts a bit like a giant, wide conveyor belt. This conveyor belt is like a flat escalator, used to move people or things across a long space. At divergent boundaries, magma pushes through, cools, and forms new crust.

The lithosphere is like a rigid board, though, and as two plates move apart, the other end of each plate collides with another lithosphere. At the collision, one plate is subducted, or pushed under, and melts. So lithosphere is created on one end, and destroyed on another. Just like conveyor belts, or the stairs on an escalator, lithosphere appears on one end and disappears on the other end.

TECTONIC HISTORY OF THE PACIFIC NORTHWEST

WORDS TO KNOW

tectonic: relating to the forces that produce movement and changes in the earth's crust.

erosion: when a surface is worn away by wind or water.

geologists: scientists who study the earth and its movements.

algae: plants that live mainly in water. They do not have leaves, roots, or stems.

sediments: loose rock particles such as sand or clay.

The Pacific Northwest has had a very active **tectonic** history. The rocks often record this history, but it can be hard to sort out what happened when. And sometimes rocks have been completely removed due to **erosion** or subduction. As you might guess, the farther back in time you go, the harder it is to tell what happened. Nevertheless, **geologists** have pieced together a rough picture of the tectonic past.

About a billion years ago, all the continents on earth were assembled into a single continent surrounded by one giant ocean. This huge supercontinent has been named Rodinia. It was a bleak place. The only plants were single-celled **algae**. There were no animals. And there were probably huge storms.

About 750 million years ago, Rodinia broke apart. The rift was about where the western edge of Idaho is today, and as the continent pulled apart, an ocean formed. The east side of the rift is now Idaho and western Montana. Some of the oldest rocks in the Pacific Northwest region can be found here. Most of what we now know as Washington and Oregon didn't exist then!

Did You Know?

Rodinia is a Russian word that means "homeland." Pangaea is a Greek word that means "all lands."

Millions of years passed, and a new supercontinent slowly formed. Scientists called this new supercontinent Pangaea. About 200 million years ago, Pangaea also broke apart and the Atlantic Ocean began to form. That pushed the North American Plate westward, where it collided with an oceanic plate. This oceanic plate began subducting beneath the North American Plate.

A BIG BASIN

When Rodinia started to break apart, a large basin started forming where the western border of Idaho is today. Huge piles of **sediments** built up in the basin. At places, these piles of sediment were 13 miles thick (21 kilometers)!

Today, rocks formed from these sediments are known as Belt rocks (named after Belt, Montana). You can find them in western Montana and northeastern Idaho. Glacier National Park has Belt rocks exposed in its beautiful mountains.

But the oceanic plate had lots of accumulated sediments on top of it. So when the oceanic crust was pushed under the North American Plate, the sediments were scraped off and they stuck onto the continent. There were also volcanoes forming from the subduction. Over many millions of years, other rocks were jammed onto the continent. All of these rocks eventually became Washington and Oregon.

Between 7 and 4 million years ago, the subduction became steeper. This means that the subducting plate pushed down at a steeper angle, and it caused the continental edge to fold. The Olympic Mountains are on the crest of that fold.

ALASKA

Alaska is even more complicated. Geologists think that only about 1 percent of Alaska is originally from the North American continent. The rest is a mixed-up crazy quilt of rock groups that have found their way into this beautiful and interesting land.

Some of these rock groups are old continental crust. Others are oceanic rocks. Some rocks formed nearby and some are from great distances. The movement of the plates has jammed one rock group after another onto the continent to slowly form Alaska.

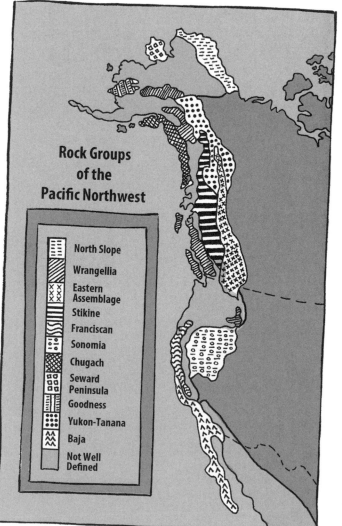

Rock Groups of the Pacific Northwest

North Slope
Wrangellia
Eastern Assemblage
Stikine
Franciscan
Sonomia
Chugach
Seward Peninsula
Goodness
Yukon-Tanana
Baja
Not Well Defined

WHAT'S HAPPENING NOW?

Right now, about 280 miles (450 kilometers) off the coast of Washington and Oregon, there is a divergent plate boundary where two oceanic plates are moving apart from each other. The plate on the eastern side of the boundary, the Juan de Fuca Plate, is being pushed farther east, where it is colliding with the continental North American Plate. And what happens when an oceanic plate meets a continental plate? Down it goes!

As it subducts, this oceanic plate partially melts, forming magma, and releasing lots of gas and steam. This is where the Cascade Mountains have formed. Because the subduction is still going on, there are many active volcanoes in the Cascades. The last major eruption from a Cascade mountain volcano was Mount St. Helens in 1980.

Subduction also causes earthquakes as the two plates lock together, then finally release with a lurch.

Meanwhile, in Alaska, another oceanic plate is subducting beneath the North American Plate. This is forming the volcanic mountains that are the Aleutian Islands. There's also a huge block of land that has been transported 375 miles in the last 30 million years (603 kilometers). As it's being jammed against the continent, it's creating Alaska's Coastal Mountains about 10 miles from the coast (16 kilometers).

MAKE YOUR OWN
SWEET PLATE BOUNDARIES

SUPPLIES

- candy bar with layers such as a Milky Way
- table knife (one that isn't sharp)
- solid chocolate candy bar

Cross Section

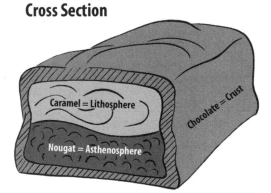

Caramel = Lithosphere

Chocolate = Crust

Nougat = Asthenosphere

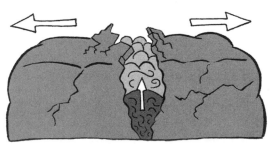

Divergent Plate Boundary

1 Cut one end from the layered candy bar—just enough to see inside. This is called the cross-section of the candy bar. How are the layers like the layers in the earth?

2 Using the knife, make two or three cracks in the chocolate across the top middle part of the layered candy bar. The chocolate on each side of the cracks represents different plates. Grab the candy bar on each end and slowly pull apart, about one inch or less. What does the gooey layer underneath do? This represents the asthenosphere, which is soft and stretches. The pulling apart represents a divergent plate boundary.

3 Push the layers back together, then push one side away from you and pull the other side towards you. Do you feel resistance? This represents a transform plate boundary, when plates grind together.

4 Take half the layered candy bar in one hand, and the solid chocolate bar in the other hand. Pretend the layered bar is a continental plate while the solid bar is an oceanic plate.

5 Push the two candy bars together, letting the solid chocolate bar go underneath the layered candy bar. This represents a convergent boundary, where two plates collide. The oceanic plate subducts beneath the continental plate.

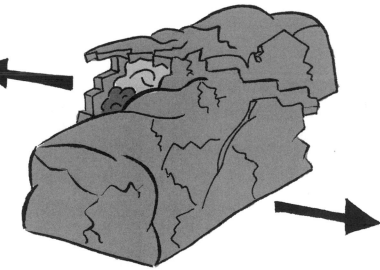

Transform Plate Boundary

PLATE TECTONICS: THE ORIGINAL RECYCLER

The earth has been recycling materials for over 4 billion years! Every rock that you see has come from another kind of rock. And every rock that you see will eventually become another one. All this recycling is because of the movement of the plates pushing everything around. To understand this recycling, first you have to know a bit about types of rocks.

There are three main types of rocks: igneous, sedimentary, and metamorphic.

Igneous Rocks have formed from the cooling of molten rock. As you go deeper beneath the surface of the earth, it becomes hotter. At around 25 miles beneath the surface, it's hot enough to melt rocks (40 kilometers). When that molten rock, called magma, comes to the surface, it cools into igneous rocks.

Sedimentary Rocks form when small particles of rock, called sediments, are pressed tightly together into rock. Sediments come from other rocks being eroded, or broken into smaller pieces by wind, water, ice, and gravity. Sedimentary rocks can also form from the remains of plants or animals being pressed together. When seawater evaporates, the minerals and salts in the water stay behind and can form into rock.

Metamorphic Rocks form when heat or pressure changes rocks into new rocks. Pressure, like temperature, increases as you go farther beneath the surface of the earth.

If rocks are pushed under the surface, but not far enough to melt, they can be changed into new rocks without first melting.

Igneous rocks can be eroded into sediments, which then form sedimentary rocks. Those sedimentary rocks can then be buried and heated and squeezed to form metamorphic rocks. Metamorphic rocks can be pushed down into the mantle and melted, to later form igneous rocks. Or it could happen in reverse, because any type of rock can form from any other type of rock.

CHAPTER 2

MOUNTAIN RANGES

The Pacific Northwest has some of the most stunning mountains in the world. These include the Coast Mountains, the Cascade Range, and the northern Rocky Mountains. Why did such beautiful mountains form here?

NORTHERN ROCKY MOUNTAINS

The Rocky Mountains, also called the Rockies, are a major mountain chain that runs from New Mexico to Canada. The northern Rockies are located in Idaho and western Montana and form the eastern boundary of the Pacific Northwest region.

The Rockies were formed around 90 million years ago. Tectonic plates slammed together, causing rocks to fold and push over each other. In geology, this is called **thrusting**. In fact, the northern Rockies are called a **fold and thrust belt** because that's how they formed.

Amazingly, the rocks that were pushed on top of the Rockies are one and a half billion years older than the rocks underneath! These older rocks are unusual because they haven't changed much. They still show original ripple marks, raindrop impressions, and mud cracks. Imagine seeing an impression of a raindrop that fell over one and a half billion years ago! These rocks can be seen throughout western Montana and Idaho, but are most spectacular in Glacier National Park in Montana.

WORDS TO KNOW

thrusting: when rocks are pushed up and over another set of rocks.

fold and thrust belt: a belt of mountains that has formed by one tectonic plate subducting under another and causing rocks farther inland to fold and be thrust over other rocks.

fossils: the remains or traces of ancient plants and animals.

glacier: a body of ice that slowly moves downhill due to gravity.

Did You Know?

Some of the rocks that have been pushed on top in the northern Rockies have many stromatolites. These are **fossils** of blue-green algae that used to live in warm, shallow seas. Many of the fossils are very detailed, and all are very old—over 1 billion years old. For geologists, it's like looking back in time.

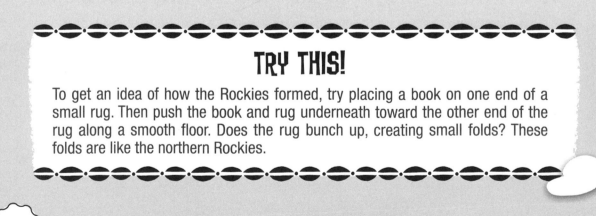

TRY THIS!

To get an idea of how the Rockies formed, try placing a book on one end of a small rug. Then push the book and rug underneath toward the other end of the rug along a smooth floor. Does the rug bunch up, creating small folds? These folds are like the northern Rockies.

THE COAST RANGE

In the last chapter, we saw how Washington and Oregon were formed when an oceanic plate subducted under the North American Plate. That oceanic plate was carrying lots of sedimentary rocks that were scraped off and squeezed and mashed and shoved upward to form stunning mountains. These mountains are called the Coast Range. It includes the Olympic Mountains to the north in Washington, the Oregon Coast Range, and the Klamath Mountains in southern Oregon and northern California.

Along the Coast Range, a peculiar type of recycling is going on.

It begins with a rock high on a mountain. Over time, this rock is eroded by rain and streams. The water carries grains of sand from the rock out into the ocean. The grains of sand settle onto the ocean floor, where they very gradually form into rock again. Meanwhile, the oceanic plate carries the rock back towards the coast. As the plate pushes under North America, the rock is scraped off and pushed higher and higher, until it's on top of the mountain again. The whole process can take 20 million years or more!

Did You Know?

The Cascades are steep and often covered with snow. They have been a barrier to people throughout history. Native American tribes were so separated by the mountains that different languages were spoken on the east and west sides.

CASCADE MOUNTAINS

The Cascade Mountains are some of the most beautiful mountains in the world. They are full of jagged peaks, **glaciers**, and waterfalls. The Cascades extend from southern Canada down through Washington, Oregon, and into northern California. They lie in a fairly straight line because they run parallel to the coast.

Did You Know?

In 1805, the Lewis and Clark Expedition found the only way to cross the Cascades was by using the Columbia River. When settlers came later following the Oregon Trail, many gave up their wagons when they came to the Cascades, and took boats down the Columbia River to reach the coast. Others took crooked, difficult trails over the mountains.

Most of the Cascades are volcanoes, and many of them are potentially still active. These snow-covered high peaks are like giants to the surrounding landscape and have inspired legends. In many Native American legends, the mountain peaks are gods that throw fire and stones at each other. Even today, the mountains are so rugged that there are huge areas far from civilization. Many people tell stories of a large, ape-like creature called Bigfoot living in the area. Another name for this creature is Sasquatch.

MOUNTAINS OF ALASKA

Alaska is a huge state, and it has huge mountains. In fact, 17 of the 20 highest peaks in North America are in Alaska, including the highest, Denali. These mountains contain an incredible array of wildlife, including grizzly bears, caribou, wolves, loons, Arctic terns, moose, and Dall sheep. There are three primary mountain ranges in Alaska.

The **Brooks Range** stretches across the entire northern part of the state from east to west. These mountains are wild and pristine. Few people live in them and they're hard to reach. The range is so far north that it's above the Arctic circle, which means that snow can fall in any month of the year. It also means that the sun does not rise on the shortest days of the year in December, and it does not set on the longest days of the year in June.

The Brooks Range is home to the Arctic National Wildlife Refuge in the east and Gates of the Arctic National Park in the central area.

Caribou

Bull Moose

20

The **Alaska Range** stretches for about 400 miles across the central part of the state (644 kilometers). These mountains are rugged and wild. The range contains several thousand glaciers that altogether occupy more area than the entire state of Connecticut! The Alaska Range contains the highest mountain in North America, Denali.

The word "Denali" means "High one" in the Athabaskan Indian language.

The **Coast Mountains** farther south extend down along the coast of Alaska and Canada. Some of these huge mountains are only 10 miles from the ocean (16 kilometers). All mountains erode, which keeps them from getting too high, but moving tectonic plates are pushing the Coast Mountains higher more quickly than they're being eroded. As a result, they are the tallest coastal mountains in the world.

Did You Know?

The Coastal Mountains in Alaska are so rugged that you often cannot travel by road from one community to another. You must go by boat or airplane. Juneau, the capital, is built on the side of a mountain!

SOME AMAZING MOUNTAINS

Denali: Also called Mt. McKinley, Denali is the highest mountain in North America at 20,320 feet (6,194 meters). It is located within Denali National Park, which is larger than the entire state of New Hampshire. From its base to its peak, Denali rises over 18,000 feet (5,486 meters). It has more bulk and more of a rise than Mt. Everest, which starts from a much higher **plateau**. And it's still rising more than an inch each year!

WORDS TO KNOW

lava: magma that has risen to the surface of the earth.

pumice: a light rock full of air spaces, formed from solidified lava.

elevation: a measurement of height above sea level.

continental United States: all of the states except for Alaska and Hawaii.

Denali is brutally cold, with temperatures as low as -40 degrees Fahrenheit (-40 degrees Celsius). It has six glaciers that are over 25 miles long (48 kilometers).

Mt. Rainier: At 14,411 feet (4,392 meters), Washington's Mt. Rainier is the highest mountain in the Cascades. It is a volcanic mountain formed from explosive eruptions with rock that cooled from **lava**, ash, mud flows, and **pumice**. Rainier is considered one of the most dangerous volcanoes in the world today. Its last eruption was 150 years ago, and it could erupt explosively again. If it did erupt, the numerous glaciers on Rainier would melt and form huge, destructive mud flows.

Mt. Rainier has 26 glaciers, the most of any single mountain in the United States. Carbon Glacier on the north side has the lowest **elevation** (3,500 feet) of any glacier in the **continental United States** (1,067 meters). Mt. Rainier's large network of caves in its glaciers formed due to hot volcanic gases and steam melting the glacial ice.

Mt. Rainier is located within Mt. Rainier National Park, which is about 50 miles southeast of Seattle (80 kilometers). With its old forests, glaciers, elk, and black bears, Mt. Rainier National Park attracts about 2 million visitors each year.

Mt. Hood: At 11,249 feet (3,429 meters), Mt. Hood is the tallest mountain in Oregon and the fourth-highest mountain in the Cascade mountain range. This explosive volcano last erupted about 170 years ago. When Lewis and Clark traveled on the Columbia River in 1805, they noted a tributary that almost blocked the Columbia due to a large sand bank.

Dall Sheep

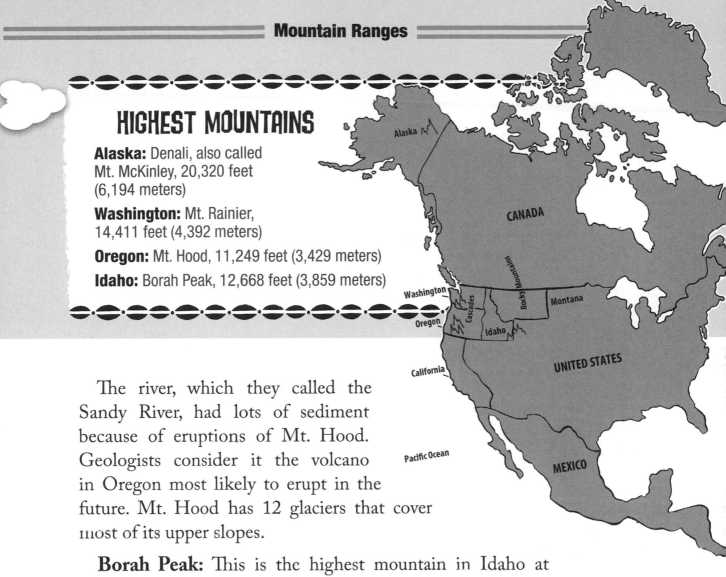

HIGHEST MOUNTAINS

Alaska: Denali, also called Mt. McKinley, 20,320 feet (6,194 meters)

Washington: Mt. Rainier, 14,411 feet (4,392 meters)

Oregon: Mt. Hood, 11,249 feet (3,429 meters)

Idaho: Borah Peak, 12,668 feet (3,859 meters)

The river, which they called the Sandy River, had lots of sediment because of eruptions of Mt. Hood. Geologists consider it the volcano in Oregon most likely to erupt in the future. Mt. Hood has 12 glaciers that cover most of its upper slopes.

Borah Peak: This is the highest mountain in Idaho at 12,668 feet (3,859 meters). It is located in a section of the northern Rockies. The mountains are rugged and dry, with little vegetation. There was a large earthquake on Borah Peak in 1983.

GLACIERS

Glaciers are like rivers of ice. To form, glaciers need two things: lots of snow and cold enough temperatures that the snow doesn't all melt in the summer. Glaciers can vary in size from a patch the size of a football field, to a "river" of ice that is a hundred miles long (161 kilometers). All of the major mountains ranges in the Pacific Northwest have glaciers.

Snow may seem light and fluffy, but when there's a lot of it, it gets heavy. As snow piles up, it presses down on the snow below, which becomes ice. Because of pressure from above, the lower layers of ice begin to flow slowly like a liquid. In addition, a thin layer of water forms underneath the ice. These two things allow the glacier to move downhill. Not very fast—usually only a few inches each day—but over time, it adds up. And sometimes, glaciers surge, or move fast—up to 100 feet in a day (30 meters)!

Did You Know?

The Taku Glacier in southern Alaska is the deepest and thickest glacier in the world outside of the polar regions. It is 4,845 feet thick (1,477 meters). Bering Glacier, also in southern Alaska, is 118 miles long (190 kilometers), which makes it the longest glacier in North America.

As a glacier moves downhill, it melts at the lower elevations where it's warmer. When more snow falls at the top of the glacier than melts at the bottom, the glacier grows. When less snow falls at the top than melts at the bottom, the glacier shrinks.

Glaciers come and go in cycles, depending on the climate.

In the last 2 million years, for example, the glaciers in Glacier National Park in Montana have formed and melted many times. The ones there today formed many thousand of years ago as the climate became colder, but are shrinking now as the climate becomes warmer.

Even though they move slowly, glaciers are extremely powerful. They crush just about anything in their path—trees, rocks, and even large boulders. As they pick up rocks and other debris, glaciers become rough like sandpaper. This roughness erodes and carves the land into U-shaped valleys and sharp mountain peaks.

Here are some things to look for that tell you a glacier has been around:

Grooves and Scratches: As the glacier drags smaller rocks over bedrock below, the smaller rocks scratch them and create grooves.

U-Shaped Valley: River valleys are V-shaped, from the river slowly cutting into the rock. Glaciers follow the path of rivers because, like rivers, they are seeking the fastest way downhill. But glaciers are wider, and the rocks they carry carve out a valley with a "U" shape.

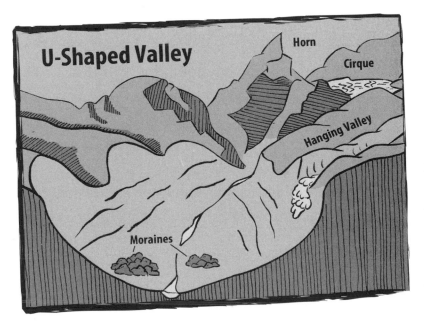

Hanging Valley: When a smaller glacier in a side canyon feeds into a larger glacier, the smaller glacier doesn't cut as deeply as the larger glacier. After they melt, the smaller glaciers leave behind smaller valleys high up on the mountainsides that look like they're hanging.

Horns: These steep-sided mountain peaks are formed by two or more glaciers carving from different directions.

Cirques: These are large bowls that form at the top, or head, of a glacier. Often the bowl fills with water, forming a small lake.

Moraines: When a glacier melts, the rocks it picked up are dumped out. Because the glacier acts like a conveyor belt made out of ice, more and more rocks are dumped out, forming a pile at the bottom and sides of the glacier. Recent moraines look like just that—a pile of rocks. Older moraines are covered by soil and plants.

Some glaciers block rivers and create temporary dams. When these dams eventually break, enormous amounts of water flood out. This is called a glacial flood.

In early June 1986, the Hubbard Glacier in southeastern Alaska moved and blocked off Russell Fiord from the sea at Disenchantment Bay. On October 8, the dam broke. It is the largest glacial flood in recorded history, with almost 3,700,000 cubic feet per second rushing into the sea (105,000 cubic meters per second). This flow was nearly 40 times as powerful as Niagara Falls and more than twice the largest recorded outflow on the Mississippi River. When was the second-largest recorded glacial lake flood? Same place, different time—August 2002. It's a busy glacier!

BOOM! ICEBERG!

When a glacier ends at the ocean, large pieces of ice break off, or "calve" into icebergs. They make loud creaking and booming sounds before breaking off. The blocks of ice can be huge—hundreds of feet high. Alaska has numerous calving glaciers. In Glacier Bay National Park in Alaska, tourists often come to watch icebergs being calved. One glacier, John Hopkins Glacier, calves such large volumes of ice that it's only safe for boats to come within about 2 miles (3 kilometers)!

Icebergs can be many different colors. White icebergs have lots of air bubbles. Blue icebergs are very dense. Greenish-black icebergs have usually calved from the bottom of the glacier. Icebergs can last for a week or more before they melt in the ocean. They make a nice resting place for passing birds. And of course what you see above the surface of the water is, as the saying goes, "only the tip of the iceberg." Most of an iceberg is below the surface of the ocean.

MAKE YOUR OWN
FOLDED MOUNTAINS

1 Using the table knife, slather the peanut butter to cover at least 2 inches of one of the pieces of cardboard (5 centimeters). The peanut butter should be at least a half-inch thick (1 centimeter).

2 Grab the opposite edge of the cardboard in one hand, and the clean piece of cardboard in the other hand. Slide the cardboard with peanut butter underneath the clean cardboard so that some of the peanut butter gloms onto the clean cardboard. Keep pushing. What shape does the peanut butter take?

What's Happening?

The clean cardboard is like continental crust, and the peanut butter cardboard is like oceanic crust with sediments (peanut butter) on top. As the oceanic crust slides under, or subducts, beneath the continental crust, the sediments attach onto the continent. The sediments often form wedges of new crust that are folded over so much that the rocks are jumbled. The Coast Range formed in this way.

SUPPLIES

- table knife (one that isn't sharp)
- peanut butter
- two pieces of cardboard at least a few inches square

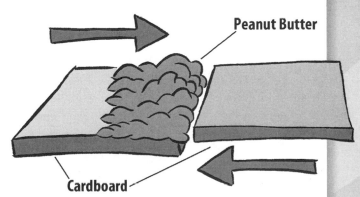

Peanut Butter

Cardboard

MAKE YOUR OWN "GLACIER"

Snow & Ice

Dirt & Pebbles

Snow & Ice

MILK

SUPPLIES

- half-gallon size paperboard milk carton
- snow or finely crushed ice
- dirt and small pebbles
- paper or plastic lunch bag
- coins or other small, heavy objects
- freezer
- scissors

1 Rinse the milk carton and open the top so it has a square opening.

2 Fill the carton with layers of snow or crushed ice, sprinkling the dirt and small pebbles in between the layers. Let the snow settle and add more snow and dirt layers until the carton is full.

3 Fill the lunch bag with about 2 inches of coins or other small, heavy objects (5 centimeters). Close the bag and place it on top of the snow. Place the carton in the freezer with the open side up.

4 Check the carton every day or so. If there's room at the top, take out the bag, add more snow and dirt/pebbles, and replace the bag.

5 After about a week, take the carton out and peel or cut the paperboard container away. If you have trouble releasing the paperboard, run it under warm water for a minute. What does the snow look like? Does it look more like snow or ice?

What's Happening?

Snow is made of ice crystals. When it is under pressure (like from the weight of the coins), the feathery snow crystals break down and recrystallize into solid ice. You may not have had enough weight and time for the snow to completely form into ice. But in a glacier, the immense weight of the snow on top causes all of the snow underneath to recrystallize as solid ice.

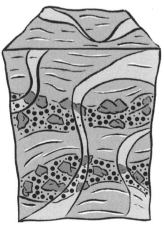

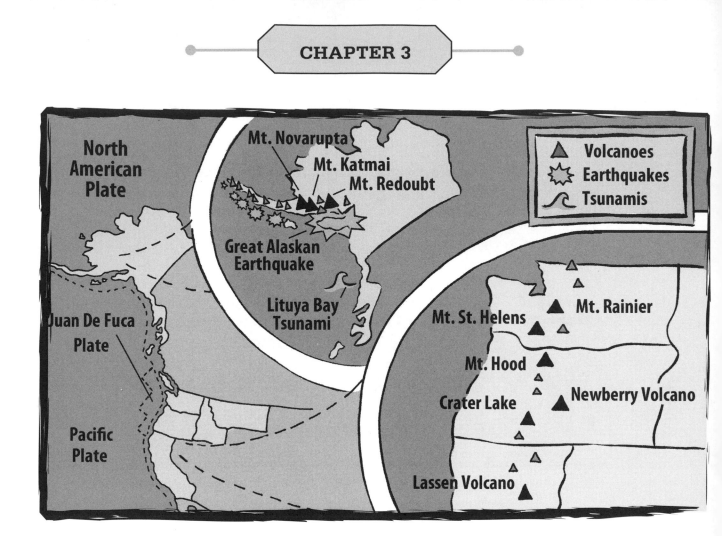

CHAPTER 3

VOLCANOES AND EARTHQUAKES!

On the surface, the Pacific Northwest seems to be a gentle land, with fog and mist and snow, and great, silent trees. But underneath, tectonic plates are pushing together. This causes **volcanoes** to erupt, **earthquakes** to tremble, and **tsunamis** to crash into beaches.

WHAT ARE VOLCANOES?

Volcanoes are formed when magma comes to the surface. Sometimes the liquid rock cools before it reaches the surface. When that happens, it forms rocks such as granite. But when the magma comes all the way to the surface before it cools, it's called lava, and it comes out through an opening in the earth called a volcano.

Lava can slowly bubble out of the earth or it can shoot out violently. What's the formula for an explosive volcano? Thick lava with lots of water vapor.

Liquids that are very **viscous**, like honey, resist flow. Less viscous liquids, like water, flow easily. If you've ever heated up a thick soup in the microwave, you may have noticed that thick liquids can sometimes have a mini-explosion, splattering soup all over the inside of the microwave. Thick lava can explode in the same way.

It also depends on how much gas, mainly water vapor, is still in the lava when it reaches the surface. Lots of dissolved gas creates pressure in the lava. This makes it more explosive, like a soda can that's been shaken. Gas is more easily trapped in more viscous lava.

WORDS TO KNOW

volcano: a vent in the earth's surface through which magma, ash, and gases erupt.

earthquake: a sudden movement in the outer layer of the earth that releases stress built up from the motion of the earth's plates.

tsunami: a series of giant waves caused by earthquakes, explosions, meteors, or landslides.

viscous: how thick and fluid a substance is. Honey is very viscous, while water is not.

Did You Know?

An active volcano is a volcano that has erupted in recorded history. Geologists think it will erupt again, probably in the next 200 years. A dormant volcano is a "sleepy" volcano that hasn't erupted in recorded history, but could erupt again. An extinct volcano is one that hasn't erupted in many thousands of years and isn't expected to erupt again.

TYPES OF VOLCANOES

WORDS TO KNOW

shield volcano: a broad volcano formed from the flow of runny, non-explosive lava.

stratovolcano: a classic cone-shaped volcano with alternating layers of runny lava flows and more explosive volcanic deposits.

cinder cone: a small, steep-sided volcano, built up by ash and small cinders.

volcanic dome: a volcano formed by thick lava oozing out. The lava is too thick to travel far and builds up into a dome.

There are four main types of volcanoes, and all of them are represented in the Pacific Northwest.

- **Shield volcanoes** are large but low, resembling a warrior's shield lying on the ground. These volcanoes erupt quietly. They slowly eject a fluid lava that can flow a long way before it cools.

- **Stratovolcanoes** are also called composite volcanoes. They have a classic volcanic cone shape and can erupt explosively. Sometimes stratovolcanoes blow off their tops. They also produce pyroclastic flows, which are deadly avalanches of extremely hot gases, ash, and rocks.

- **Cinder cones** are small, steep-sided hills that have a classic volcano shape. They are built up by cinders that were ejected and cooled while flying through the air. When they're actually erupting, cinder cones look like a lava fountain.

- **Volcanic domes** happen when lava that is too thick to flow oozes out of a volcano. It slowly builds up into a volcanic dome.

Cross Section of Shield Volcano

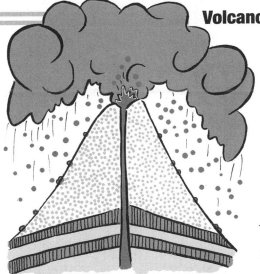

Cross Section of Cinder Cone Volcano

It's a bit like toothpaste where the cap is left off and the toothpaste dries out. That might sound slow and boring, but the pressure can build up and make these volcanoes very explosive.

Volcanoes can also form in rift zones where tectonic plates are pulling or rifting apart. The crust cracks, and magma pushes out. Rift zones often produce flat, thick plateaus of cooled lava.

PACIFIC NORTHWEST VOLCANOES

In the Pacific Northwest, many volcanoes have formed because of the Pacific Plate pushing under the North American continent. The Cascades have over 2,300 volcanoes that have erupted in the last 2 million years. The United States Geological Survey closely monitors 13 of these volcanoes because they are considered a threat.

Alaska is also full of volcanoes. More than 40 volcanoes have erupted since the mid-1700s, and up to 100 volcanoes have erupted in the last 2 million years. Alaska's Aleutian Islands are a chain of more than 300 small volcanic islands.

Did You Know?

In 1989 a jet airplane was flying over an active volcano called Mount Redoubt in western Alaska. The volcano started erupting and spewed an ash plume 45,000 feet high (13,716 meters). The ash melted as it hit the hot engines, coating them with glass. The engines stopped and the plane started falling. Luckily, the pilots were able to restart the engines just before crashing.

Cross Section of Lava Dome Volcano

33

WORDS TO KNOW

landslide: rock and earth sliding down a slope due to gravity.

lahar: a mudflow that forms from lava and ash mixing with melted snow and rain. It can wipe out everything in its path.

Here are some of the best-known volcanoes in the Pacific Northwest:

Mount St. Helens erupted on May 18, 1980, in the deadliest and most destructive volcanic eruption in United States history. This large, stratovolcano located in Washington is part of the Cascade Mountains. Its catastrophic eruption caused an enormous **landslide** and killed 57 people. Trees, bridges, railways, highways, and homes were destroyed for hundreds of miles around.

As early as 1978, members of the U.S. Geological Survey began to see signs that the volcano might erupt soon. They began closely monitoring the volcano. In 1980, a 450-foot-high bulge developed on the north side of the volcano. This told geologists that magma was building up. On March 27, 1980, steam began erupting from the volcano and people were evacuated.

There was an earthquake on May 18, 1980, at 8:32 a.m. Seconds after the earthquake, the bulge broke loose, causing the largest landslide in recorded history. An explosive blast of steam, hot gas, rock, and bits of lava screamed down the volcano at 680 miles per hour (1,100 kilometers). That's faster than a jet airplane!

Cross Section of Stratovolcano

A cloud of ash rose 15 miles into the sky (24 kilometers) for nine hours. The day turned dark, and ash was carried across the western United States.

The hot lava and gas melted the snow, and mixed together with rock. This **lahar** raced down the side of the volcano and destroyed 200 homes. So much mud flowed down the Columbia River that 31 ships were stranded in ports on the river.

Mount St. Helens is still active, with much smaller eruptions occurring. The last eruption started in 2004 and lasted about four years. In 1982, the Mount St. Helens National Volcanic Monument was established for research, recreation, and education.

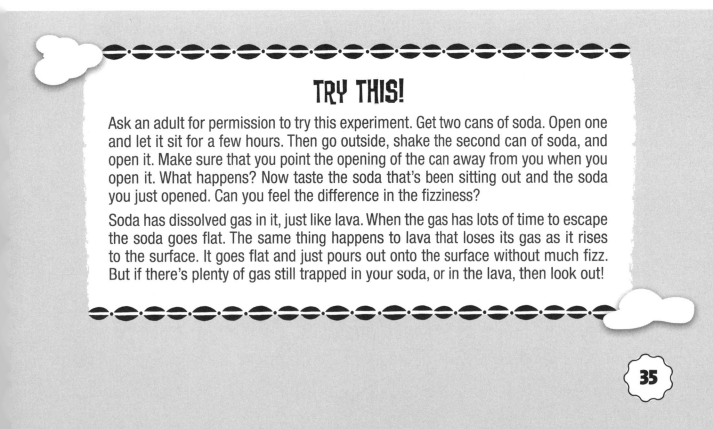

TRY THIS!

Ask an adult for permission to try this experiment. Get two cans of soda. Open one and let it sit for a few hours. Then go outside, shake the second can of soda, and open it. Make sure that you point the opening of the can away from you when you open it. What happens? Now taste the soda that's been sitting out and the soda you just opened. Can you feel the difference in the fizziness?

Soda has dissolved gas in it, just like lava. When the gas has lots of time to escape the soda goes flat. The same thing happens to lava that loses its gas as it rises to the surface. It goes flat and just pours out onto the surface without much fizz. But if there's plenty of gas still trapped in your soda, or in the lava, then look out!

GEOLOGY OF THE PACIFIC NORTHWEST

WORDS TO KNOW

caldera: a bowl-like depression at the top of a volcano. It forms when the magma chamber underneath is emptied and collapses.

Mt. Rainier is considered one of the most dangerous volcanoes in the world. Mt. Rainier is a Decade Volcano, which means that it's one of the 16 volcanoes around the world that could cause the greatest destruction and loss of life. The name Decade Volcano comes from the program to identify these destructive volcanoes, which was part of the International Decade for Natural Disaster Reduction.

Mt. Rainier is so dangerous because it is an explosive volcano and it has huge amounts of glacial ice. The hot steam and lava would melt the ice and mix with it to form lahars. These mudflows can travel up to 40 miles per hour (64 kilometers) and wipe out anything in their path. In the distant past, Mt. Rainier's mudflows reached as far away as Seattle, but few people lived there then. Now, there are large populations of people who live in the path of these mudflows. Even though Mt. Rainier last erupted about 150 years ago, it's still an active volcano and could erupt again. Geologists monitor volcanoes like Mt. Rainier so they can warn people before they erupt.

LAVA TUBES!

When rivers of molten lava run underground, they make channels, or caves. These are called lava tubes. You can see lots of lava tubes in Lava Beds National Monument in northeastern California. There are more than 700 lava tube caves, many with ladders and trails. The longest lava tube in the continental United States is Ape Cave in Mount St. Helens National Monument. It's almost 2½ miles long (4 kilometers)!

Crater Lake isn't a volcano, but it sits on top of one. Mt. Mazama is a stratovolcano located in Oregon's Cascade Range. It was the site of an enormous eruption 7,700 years ago. This eruption was even bigger than the 1980 eruption of Mount St. Helens, expelling as much as 50 to 100 times more material. Mt. Mazama erupted many times after that, and eventually the chamber that held the magma underneath collapsed. A **caldera**, or bowl-like depression, formed at the top of the volcano. The caldera later filled with rainwater and snowmelt to form Crater Lake.

Did You Know?

One way to tell if a volcano is active or not is by its shape. Older, inactive volcanoes are more jagged, because glaciers have had plenty of time to erode the mountain. Active volcanoes, which have erupted and formed more recently, tend to have a smoother look.

If you think a lake at the top of a mountain must be small, think again. Crater Lake is 5 miles across (8 kilometers) and up to 1,949 feet deep (594 meters). It is the ninth-deepest lake in the world, and the deepest lake that is entirely within the United States.

Newberry Volcano is one of the most famous shield volcanoes in the Pacific Northwest. Tall, explosive volcanoes like Mount St. Helens only account for about 25 percent of the lava that has flowed in the Pacific Northwest from volcanoes (not including eruptions called flood basalts that you will learn about in chapter 4). Most of the lava has come from shield volcanoes. These quietly eject a runny lava that can spread far and wide.

Did You Know?

Newberry Volcano has lots of **obsidian** in its center. This volcanic glass is used to make surgical instruments sharper than steel. Obsidian was traded by Native Americans throughout the Pacific Northwest.

Newberry Volcano is the biggest volcano in Oregon, if you're measuring the amount of lava spewed. It is also one of the largest shield volcanoes in the continental United States: 40 miles long (64 kilometers) and 20 miles wide (32 kilometers), with a crater 4 miles wide (6 kilometers)!

Newberry Volcano last erupted 1,300 years ago. This eruption is known as the Big Obsidian Flow. If you took the volume of rock in this flow and made a paved road with it 6 inches thick (15 centimeters) and 24 feet wide (7 meters), it would circle the earth three times! Geologists think there is a chamber of magma about 2 or 3 miles beneath the surface (3 to 5 kilometers), and it could erupt again. Scientists are exploring how the heat from this magma, known as geothermal energy, can be used to generate electricity.

Mt. Novarupta and Mt. Katmai are two stratovolcanoes where the largest volcanic eruption of the century happened in Alaska in 1912. They released 30 times the volume of magma as Mount St. Helens' eruption. Ash spread all over the world and caused roofs to collapse in Alaska.

WORDS TO KNOW

obsidian: dark volcanic glass formed when lava cools so fast it can't form crystals.

fault: a crack in the outer layer of the earth where the rocks have moved past one another.

Richter scale: the scale for measuring the strength of an earthquake.

A valley near the volcanoes received hundreds of feet of ash. This ash was white-hot, up to 2,000 degrees Fahrenheit (1,093 degrees Celsius). The valley's river turned into steam, which escaped through cracks, causing thousands of "smokes." This area became known as the Valley of Ten Thousand Smokes. It covers 40 square miles (104 square kilometers) and is filled with ash up to 700 feet deep (213 meters). The Valley of Ten Thousand Smokes is now part of the Katmai National Park and Preserve.

EARTHQUAKES!

When stress builds up in rocks, they can suddenly lurch into a new position. That lurching is called an earthquake. Most earthquakes happen along **faults**, which are cracks in the lithosphere, and especially at plate boundaries. You might expect there to be earthquakes in the Pacific Northwest because of the plate boundaries located there. You would be right.

In the Pacific Northwest, there are four types of earthquakes. All of them are related to the oceanic Juan de Fuca Plate pushing underneath the continental North American Plate. Earthquakes can occur within the Juan de Fuca Plate, within the North American Plate, between the two plates, or by rising magma as it cracks the colder rock above.

Did You Know?

Earthquakes are measured mainly by their magnitude. Magnitude is the strength of the earthquake and is recorded on the Richter scale. The **Richter scale** is a logarithmic scale. This means that when the measurement increases by 1, the magnitude increases by 10. So an earthquake that measures 8.0 is 10 times as powerful as an earthquake that measures 7.0.

WHAT DOES AN EARTHQUAKE FEEL LIKE?

Here are some typical effects that people might feel near the epicenter of earthquakes of various magnitudes. The epicenter is the point on the earth's surface that is directly above the location of an earthquake.

Magnitude on the Richter Scale	What it Feels Like	How Often They Occur in the World
Below 3.0	People usually can't feel it.	1,000 per day
3.0 to 3.9	People can feel a slight trembling, but there is no damage.	Over 100 per day
4.0 to 4.9	Tables and chairs rattle.	About 20 per day
5.0 to 6.9	Some damage to buildings, especially if they're poorly built.	About 3 per day
7.0 to 7.9	Serious damage to buildings, with some destroyed.	18 per year
8.0 to 8.9	Serious damage for several hundred miles.	1 per year
9.0 to 9.9	Devastating, affecting people for thousands of miles.	1 per 20 years
10.0 and up	Never recorded.	?

Earthquakes can occur as deep as 30 miles beneath the surface of the earth (48 kilometers), or they can happen much nearer to the surface. The biggest earthquakes occur where the two plates have been locked together for hundreds of years, then finally release in an extra-large snap. Nearly 17,000 earthquakes of magnitude 1.0 to 6.0 have been recorded in Oregon and Washington since 1970. About 15 to 20 earthquakes per year are felt in the Pacific Northwest.

ALASKAN EARTHQUAKES

The 1964 Great Alaskan Earthquake occurred on March 27, 1964, in Prince William Sound near Anchorage, Alaska. It measured 9.2 on the Richter scale. There was much damage to buildings and roads and 131 people died. The land moved vertically by as much as 49 feet (15 meters). It generated a huge tsunami wave 230 feet high (70 meters), one of the largest tsunamis ever recorded.

The Great Alaskan Earthquake is the most powerful earthquake ever recorded in North America, and the second-most powerful ever recorded in the world. The largest was a 9.5 earthquake in Chile in 1960.

Fourth Avenue
Anchorage, Alaska
March 29, 1964
2 Days After the Great Quake

MIMA MOUNDS MYSTERY...

Some of the most mysterious natural formations in the Pacific Northwest are called "mima mounds." These are mounds of earth up to 6 feet high and about 30 feet across (2 meters high and 9 meters across). They are found in eastern Washington, but no one knows for sure how they got there.

But whenever there's a mystery, scientists have theories:

- They were built by prairie dogs.
- They arose from cracking in the soil due to drying or frost.
- They grew as sediment blown by the wind clumped around vegetation.
- They were formed by glaciers.
- They were formed by earthquakes.

The last theory came to a man named Andrew Berg while he was building a doghouse. He was using plywood that was coated with fine volcanic ash. As he pounded away, he noticed that the ash formed into small bumps of ash, remarkably like the mima mounds. He figured that vibrations on a much larger scale, like from an earthquake, could create the mima mounds.

Think About It!

Earthquakes and volcanoes tend to occur in similar locations. Why do you think this is the case?

WORDS TO KNOW

wavelength: the distance from crest to crest in a series of waves.

Another enormous earthquake in Alaska occurred on November 3, 2002. The Denali earthquake in Denali National Park, measured 7.9 on the Richter scale. The earth's surface was ruptured for 209 miles (336 kilometers)! The earthquake created waves in Lake Union in Seattle, Washington, that damaged boats. There were thousands of landslides in and around Denali, but no one died because few people live in the area.

The trans-Alaskan oil pipeline, which carries oil from the Arctic Ocean to the southern edge of Alaska, crosses the Denali fault. The pipeline carries huge amounts of oil, and if it had broken there could have been terrible environmental effects. But the pipeline had been designed so that it could "slide" on beams during an earthquake. As a result, the pipeline wasn't damaged.

TSUNAMI!

When an earthquake occurs beneath an ocean, and the ocean floor moves up or down, it pushes the water up or down quickly. This creates a series of giant waves called a tsunami. Tsunamis can also be caused by underwater explosions, meteorites, or landslides.

Way out at sea, tsunamis are only a foot high—not even enough for a ship to notice. The **wavelength** can be very long though, sometimes up to 120 miles from one crest of the wave to the next (193 kilometers).

Did You Know?

The largest wave ever recorded in the world occurred on July 9, 1958 in Lituya Bay, Alaska. An earthquake caused a large amount of rock to plunge into the bay, generating the wave. The tsunami wiped out trees as high as 1,720 feet above sea level (524 meters). That's higher than the Empire State Building!

Tsunamis travel as fast as a jet airplane. But when they approach the coast, the waves slow down, bunch up, and become very high. One warning sign that a tsunami is coming is that the water often dramatically recedes, or draws back, before the waves arrive.

Tsunamis can travel across entire oceans with devastating effects. In 1960, the earthquake in Chile generated a tsunami that traveled over 10,000 miles in 22 hours (16,093 kilometers). When it hit Japan, 150 people were killed from the huge amount of water.

Did You Know?

In 2004, ten-year-old Tilly Smith was with her parents at the beach in Thailand. She had learned about tsunamis in her school geography class. She saw that the water was pulling back, and told her parents that a tsunami was coming. They warned others and saved many lives.

MAKE YOUR OWN
MIMA MOUNDS

1 Set the foam core board outside, on top of the bricks, with one brick on each end. Spread the flour out evenly on the board until you can't see the board underneath.

2 From underneath, gently tap the board with the spoon over and over. Do you see the flour forming into mounds? Try tapping the board in different places. Does it change the mounds? Smooth the flour out and try different thicknesses of flour. Does it affect the shape or spacing of the mounds?

SUPPLIES

- sheet of foam core board at least 2 by 2 feet (⅔ by ⅔ meter)
- 2 bricks
- 2 cups or more of flour or cornstarch (½ liter)
- large spoon

What's Happening?

Your tapping is like an earthquake vibrating the earth. The mima mounds could have formed from loose soil, like your flour, vibrating over a hard surface like rock underneath.

MAKE YOUR OWN
TSUNAMI

1 Fill the bathtub with water 1 or 2 inches deep at the shallow end (2½ to 5 centimeters).

2 Place the board flat under the water at the faucet end of the bathtub. With one hand, hold down the side of board away from the faucet. With your other hand, quickly lift the side of the board closest to the faucet.

3 Observe the wave you created as it goes toward the other end of the bathtub. Does it change as it reaches the end? If you add more water to the bathtub, does the wave change?

SUPPLIES

- bathtub
- thin, stiff board about 8 by 10 inches (20 by 25 centimeters)

What's Happening?

When you quickly snap the board up, it acts like the earth under the ocean during an earthquake. An earthquake that occurs under the ocean causes waves that aren't very high, but are very broad. As the waves approach the land, they bunch up and the waves become much higher. Your bathtub isn't nearly big enough to cause such giant waves, but did you notice the waves bunching up a bit as they came to the end of the bathtub?

CHAPTER 4

BASINS AND PLATEAUS

If you had x-ray vision like Superman, you could stand on the Cascade Mountains and see a vast, relatively flat area of black rock stretching east all the way to the Rocky Mountains. Some of it would be covered by soil and some of it would be exposed to the air. But to your x-ray eyes, it would look a bit like a black ocean.

WORDS TO KNOW

basalt: a black, shiny volcanic rock.

Columbia Intermontane: the relatively flat area in Washington, Oregon, and Idaho between the Cascade and Rocky Mountains.

vent: an opening in the earth's crust where molten lava and volcanic gases escape. Also called a fissure.

flood basalt: a giant flow or a series of very large flows of lava that form basalt rocks.

fine-grained: rock that has mineral grains that are too small to see.

This black rock is called **basalt**, and this stretch of it is located in the **Columbia Intermontane**. An intermontane is the area between mountain ranges. The Columbia Intermontane covers a huge area in the center of the Pacific Northwest—over 100,000 square miles across Washington, Oregon, Idaho, and a small area of northern Nevada (259,000 square kilometers).

COLUMBIA INTERMONTANE

The Columbia Intermontane really did used to be a kind of ocean—an ocean of hot lava flows. These flows weren't just dribbles of lava. They were HUGE flows of lava pouring out of volcanoes over and over. There was so much lava that it didn't cool very quickly and could flow for months and even years, covering great distances. Some of the lava flowed into the ocean, even though it was hundreds of miles away from the **vents**.

Because of how it was formed, the basalt in this area is called **flood basalt**. The entire area is now referred to as the Columbia River Basalts. The Columbia Intermontane has one of the world's largest areas of continental flood basalts. These huge floods of lava buried older rocks, creating vast lava plains.

Did You Know?

The Columbia Intermontane is sometimes called the Columbia Plateau. Compared to the large mountains to the east and west of it, the Columbia Plateau is relatively flat. But it still has ridges and valleys, hills and terraces.

The first flooding filled in valleys, then later floods deposited thinner, flat sheets of basalts. There are many wonderful places to view the basalt of the Columbia Intermontane. One of them is Multnomah Falls, a waterfall on the Oregon side of the Columbia River Gorge. You can see five different flows of basalt on the cliff face of the waterfall.

Did You Know?

Alaska also has an intermontane plateau located between the Brooks Range and the Alaska Range. It's called the Central Plateau and it's the largest geographic region in Alaska. It's even larger than the state of Texas!

BASALT

Basalt is an igneous rock that forms when certain types of lava flows onto the surface of the earth. It's dark gray to black and very **fine-grained**. Basalt is quite dense, or heavy, because its minerals are dense. It is the most common type of rock on earth, but most basalt is located on the ocean's floors. The Columbia Plateau has one of the largest areas of basalt on a continent.

When basalt lava erupts and cools, it shrinks and cracks. Often, the cracks are very regular and the basalt forms into vertical columns that have 5, 6, or 7 sides.

Sometimes basalt lava flows from a central vent or opening, and forms a cone—what we call a volcano. But basalt lava can also flow quietly out from long openings in the earth, called fissures or vents. This lava is not very viscous, which means that it flows easily. The flood basalts flowed out of long vents.

Lava

Magma Fissure

Hardened Igneous Basalt Layers

THE COLUMBIA RIVER BASALTS

There are many interesting facts about the Columbia River Basalts.

• The lava that formed the basalts flowed out of fissures 15 to 30 feet wide (5 to 10 meters). There were perhaps as many as 20,000 fissures, some as long as 150 miles (240 kilometers). The lava flowed out as fast as 3 miles per hour (5 kilometers), faster than most animals can run for long periods.

• A total of about 63,000 square miles (163,799 square kilometers) were covered by flood basalts. That's an area larger than most states in the United States.

• The basalt rock has a volume of about 41,820 cubic miles (179,000 cubic kilometers) and perhaps even more. If you cut the basalt into 1-foot cubes and stacked those cubes from the earth to the sun, you would have 12,816 towers!

• In some places, the basalt is more than a mile thick (1½ kilometers).

WORDS TO KNOW

livestock: animals raised for food or other products.

plume of magma: a large area of magma that rises to the surface from deep in the mantle. It has an upside-down teardrop shape.

delaminate: when the lower part splits off.

THE LARGEST LAVA FLOWS

In 1783 there was an eruption from a fissure in Iceland that lasted eight months and produced 3 cubic miles of lava (12 cubic kilometers). It was the largest lava flow in recorded history. It also produced poisonous clouds that killed more than half of the country's **livestock**. Over 10,000 people died in Iceland, mostly from starvation, and there was famine around the world. But as huge as the Iceland eruption was, the eruptions that spewed out the Columbia River Basalts were much greater. The Columbia basalt flows were over 100 times greater in volume, and they happened over and over!

• The Columbia River Basalts are the youngest flood basalts on earth. This means they have experienced less erosion than other flood basalts. As a result, these basalts have been studied more than any other flood basalts in the world.

• The lava erupted between 17 million and 6 million years ago. Most of the eruptions occurred in the first 1½ million years of that period.

WHAT CAUSES FLOOD BASALTS?

Flood basalts are unusual. They only occur about once every 50 million years or so, and they don't usually happen near plate boundaries. Geologists have different theories for how and why flood basalts are produced, and over such a large area.

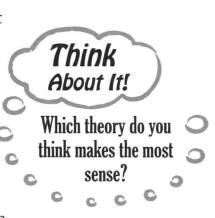

Think About It!

Which theory do you think makes the most sense?

The Plume Theory—the "Big Balloon"—proposes that a giant, abnormally hot **plume of magma** rises from deep in the earth. It melts rock as it rises. These plumes are so big that when they break through the crust, spilling lava, they can be 500 miles across (800 kilometers).

The Delamination Theory—the "Super Sandwich"—proposes that flood basalts occur when the lithosphere **delaminates**, and sinks down into the mantle. Think of the lithosphere as a sandwich. If you peel away the bottom piece of bread, or lithosphere, it allows lots of the hotter, gooier asthenosphere below to push up and melt the rock above. It pours out as flood basalts.

The Plume and Delamination Theory—Big Balloon Meets Super Sandwich—combines the two. A plume of magma rises from the mantle and melts the lower lithosphere to start the flood basalts. While the plume moves up, the lower lithosphere begins delaminating, producing even more basalt eruptions.

WORDS TO KNOW

Ice Age: a period of time when glaciers covered a large part of the earth's surface.

scablands: an area with deep, dry channels and rough, gouged rocks.

MEGA FLOOD!

Around 16,000 years ago, near the end of the last **Ice Age**, the area between Idaho and the Cascade Mountains experienced the largest known flood of freshwater. The floods gouged huge channels from the earth, and left the basalt rocks broken, jagged, and jumbled. This area is now called the Channeled **Scablands**, because it is like a scab on the earth. What happened to cause such massive flooding?

Glacial Lake Missoula was a massive lake in western Montana formed by a glacier that dammed the Clark Fork River. The lake was about 2,000 feet deep (610 meters) and more than 200 miles long (322 kilometers). It held more water than Lake Erie and Lake Ontario combined. When enough water had built up behind the ice dam, the pressure from the water broke through the ice all at once, causing the flooding.

The floods that followed were unlike anything seen in modern history. If you took the flow of all the rivers in the world right now, the amount of water per hour shooting out from Glacial Lake Missoula would be 10 times as much as all of them combined.

Flood water raced across the landscape at 65 miles per hour (105 kilometers). It swept away hundreds of feet of soil and cut deep canyons in the earth. The lake was drained in about two days. Amazingly, the glacier continued to form again and again. At least 13 and perhaps 70 floods occurred.

SNAKE RIVER PLAIN

The Snake River Plain is a flat, 400-mile-long depression containing basalt rocks. It stretches across southern Idaho and covers about a quarter of the state. The Snake River Plain is home to most of Idaho's major cities and agricultural land.

Many geologists think that the Snake River Plain was formed from the same plume of magma that caused the Columbia River Basalts. That plume has moved and is now under Yellowstone National Park at the very eastern end of the Snake River Plain.

The Snake River Plain contains many fascinating geological features, including the Great Rift Zone. This large area of fractures, or breaks in the earth's crust, is about 50 miles long (80 kilometers). It's the largest rift zone in the United States. Here, the crust is literally pulling apart, or rifting.

Did You Know?

The National Park Service has proposed an Ice Age Floods National Geologic Trail. To read more, go to www.iafi.org/trail.html. This trail system would bring the dramatic story of the Ice Age Floods to the public.

The lava flowing in this area is so new that there's very little vegetation.

One of the main features of the Great Rift Zone is the King's Bowl Rift. Its main fissure is about 6 to 8 feet wide (2 to 2½ meters) and in some areas you can actually descend into the rift several hundred feet. The deepest rift crack in the world is located here and it's 800 feet deep (244 meters)! The Great Rift Zone also contains Craters of the Moon National Monument and Preserve. It has spectacular and strange volcanoes, ropy basalt, and lava tubes. President Calvin Coolidge, who declared it a National Monument in 1924, called it "a weird and scenic landscape peculiar to itself."

PERSEVERANCE PAYS OFF

Most landforms are shaped over thousands or even millions of years. Erosion usually takes a very long time. So geologists used to think that the Channeled Scablands were gouged out and formed by rivers and glaciers over millions of years. Then, in the 1920s, a geologist named J Harlen Bretz started looking closer at the rocks and puzzling out how this landscape had formed.

WORDS TO KNOW

ripple marks: parallel ridges formed from flowing water or air.

When Bretz first visited the area, few geologists had ever been there. Bretz saw evidence that didn't add up. Huge boulders had been transported from distant places. Glaciers can transport large boulders, but the glaciers hadn't come that far south. So what had moved them?

Also, there were riverbed channels that were so deep they must have had huge amounts of water flowing through them, but they were now dry. Another geologist found **ripple marks**, like what you find in sand at the ocean or in a river. But these ripple marks were huge: up to 50 feet high (15 meters) and 500 feet apart (150 meters). Such giant ripple marks could only have formed from a huge amount of water moving fast.

Bretz proposed that giant floods had caused the scablands. Other geologists scoffed. They called Bretz and his ideas "preposterous" and "incompetent."

Bretz must have been tempted to give up on his research in the scablands. But he knew that his research was sound. He had checked his own work, thought it through and re-thought. His ideas were the only ones that explained everything he was seeing.

By the 1950s, Bretz's ideas were finally accepted by other geologists. In 1979, at the age of 96, Bretz received the Penrose Medal, the highest award in geology.

In science, as in much else, there is no substitute for seeing something with your own eyes, and coming to your own conclusions. That's what J Harlen Bretz did. And he changed the way we think about a huge area in the Pacific Northwest, and even geology itself.

Think About It!

Do you know of any other instances where everyone thought they KNEW the truth, but were actually mistaken? What does it take to discover the truth?

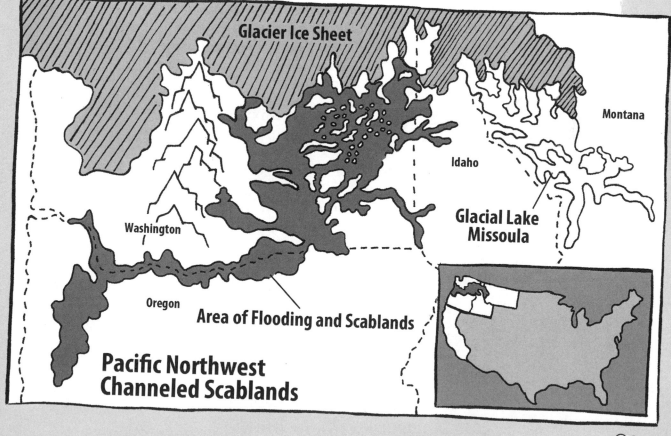

Glacier Ice Sheet

Montana

Idaho

Glacial Lake Missoula

Washington

Oregon

Area of Flooding and Scablands

Pacific Northwest Channeled Scablands

MAKE YOUR OWN
MAGMA AND BASALT COLUMNS

Scientists use cornstarch and water to study how basalt forms into columns. You can try the same thing. The only difference between what you do and what scientists do is that they have powerful microscopes to examine what is happening.

Oobleck Under Pressure

SUPPLIES

- bright light (100 watts or brighter) or sunny windowsill
- newspaper
- 1 cup cornstarch (¼ liter)
- pie pan, ideally clear glass
- 1 cup warm tap water (¼ liter)
- spoon (optional)
- food coloring (optional)

1 Ask your parents if you can use a bright light for about one week. Or you can use a sunny windowsill where your project won't be disturbed.

2 Put newspaper on the floor, or start the project outside. Put the cornstarch in the pie pan. Slowly add water, mixing with your fingers or a spoon until all the cornstarch is wet. Mix enough so the pan is about half full. Add food coloring if you like.

3 Your mixture is called oobleck. It's fun to play with—try slapping it hard, then slowly sinking your fingers into it. Make a ball of the oobleck, pressing your hands firmly together so that the ball feels hard. Then open your hands. What happens? You can adjust your oobleck by adding a little more cornstarch if it feels too wet, or more water if it feels too powdery.

4 When you're done playing with the oobleck, place it back in the pan and wash your hands. Set the pie pan at least several inches under a bright light, or on a sunny windowsill. Wait at least one week, or until it is completely dry. You will begin to see cracks that break the cornstarch into disconnected shapes. Keep the cornstarch under the light until you see much finer cracks at the top. The longer you wait, the better.

No Pressure on Oobleck

5 If your pie pan is clear, hold it up and look at the bottom. Do you see any shapes? Carefully pry up pieces of cornstarch. Did the cornstarch form columns? Do they have a particular shape? If you don't see columns, wait longer for the cornstarch to dry out more. If you'd like to try the whole process again, just add water!

What's Happening?

When you roll oobleck around, you put a lot of pressure on the mixture and it acts like a solid. But when you open your hand, the pressure is gone and oobleck acts like a liquid. This is what happens to a plume of magma. When it's deep in the earth, it is under a LOT of pressure and it acts like a solid, moving upward maybe a few inches a year. But as it gets close to the surface of the earth, the pressure is much less, and the magma partially melts. When oobleck dries out, it acts like lava when it cools. Most liquids (except water) shrink when they cool and become solid. Lava does too. Have you ever seen mud when it dries? Does it have cracks?

MAKE YOUR OWN
MAGMA PLUMES

What makes plumes of magma rise? Try this experiment to find out.

1 Pour the water into the jar until it is a little more than half full.

2 Pour the oil into the jar and let the water and oil separate and settle. You can add food coloring if you like.

3 Shake the salt onto the oil for several seconds, or until some of the oil begins to sink. When the oil begins to rise again, you can shake salt onto it again. Keep going as long as you like!

SUPPLIES

- clear glass or plastic jar
- tap water, about 1 cup (¼ liter)
- cooking oil, about ½ cup (⅛ liter)
- food coloring (optional)
- salt in a shaker

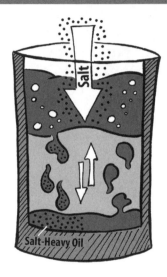

What's Happening?

Oil is less dense than water, so it weighs less. That means it floats. But salt is denser than either oil or water, so it sinks. When you shake salt onto the oil, at first it carries the oil with it. But soon the salt dissolves in the water. Without the salt to weigh it down, the oil rises again—until you shake more salt on it!

Hot materials, like magma, are also less dense than rock. They are like the oil in this experiment. Plumes of magma rise because they are hotter, and weigh less, than the surrounding rock.

CHAPTER 5

CLIMATE

The weather in the Pacific Northwest can be calm and mild. It is often the most gentle weather in the United States. But in the blink of an eye it can change dramatically to severe blizzards and winds that can tear the roofs off houses. Not only that, the weather can be totally different just a few miles away. The more you look at the weather in the Pacific Northwest, the more it changes!

WEATHER AND CLIMATE: WHAT'S THE DIFFERENCE?

People often get weather and climate confused. Weather is what happens in the atmosphere related to temperature, **precipitation**, wind, and clouds. Climate is the average weather of a place over a long period of time.

WHAT MAKES THE WEATHER?

The sun is the energy source that powers nearly everything in our world. Without the sun, the earth would not have light, heat, food, or life. Pretty bleak. It also wouldn't have weather.

WORDS TO KNOW

precipitation: rain, snow, or any other form of water that falls to Earth.

latitude: the angle of a location from the equator. The latitude is 0 degrees at the equator and 90 degrees at the North and South Poles.

The sun's energy heats our world and affects the temperature of an area. It also keeps the atmosphere in constant motion by heating up some parts more than others. This creates wind and affects clouds and precipitation.

The biggest factor in how much energy the earth receives from the sun is the angle at which the sun's rays hit the ground. When the sun is high in the sky, then the rays hit directly. But when the sun is low in the sky, the rays hit at an angle. The same energy is spread out over a larger area. That's why you feel more heat from the sun at noon, when it is overhead, than just before the sun sets.

Places that are near the equator are at a low **latitude**. These areas get very direct sunlight and are hot. But as you go farther north or south from the equator, to higher latitudes, the sun gives off less energy. This is because its rays hit at more of an angle, so it's colder.

FACTORS THAT AFFECT CLIMATE

There are four major factors that determine an area's climate. The latitude of the Pacific Northwest is about halfway between the equator and the North Pole. This is called a temperate zone. The weather varies quite a bit from season to season in a temperate zone, but is generally not too hot or too cold. Alaska is much farther from the equator, and so its climate is much colder.

Nearness to oceans is another factor affecting weather and climate. The temperature of the Pacific Ocean doesn't change too much with the seasons. This is because water, especially a large body of water like the ocean, heats up and cools down much more slowly than air or land. So if you live near the ocean you'll probably experience temperatures that are less extreme than land farther inland.

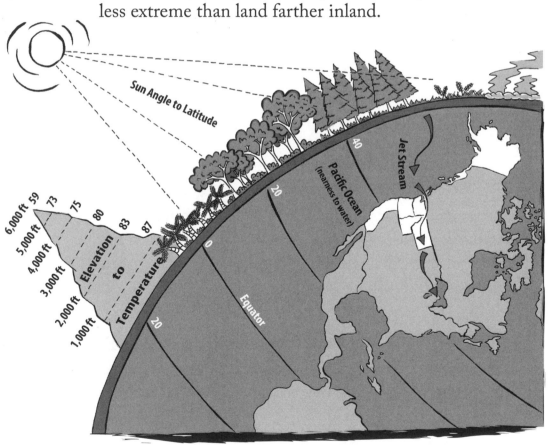

The higher you go, the colder it becomes. This is because the atmosphere acts like a blanket to keep heat in. At higher elevations, there aren't as many air molecules, so the "blanket" isn't as thick and heat escapes. That's why many high mountains are always covered in snow. It never gets warm enough up there for the snow to completely melt, even in the summer.

Weather systems, such as storms, often follow jet streams, which act just like a "highway" for storms!

Jet streams are narrow currents of air high above the surface of the earth. Jet streams have nothing to do with airplanes, but they do travel fast. They often travel as fast as 250 miles per hour (400 kilometers). There's one above the Northern Hemisphere that generally travels from west to east. It meanders north and south like a river, often traveling over the states of Washington and Oregon.

RAIN! RAIN! RAIN!

The Pacific Northwest has the reputation of being a very rainy part of the country. But the region doesn't receive more rain in a year than other parts of the United States. For example, Seattle, Washington, receives on average about 38 inches of rain per year (97 centimeters). That's less than Boston (44 inches/112 centimeters), Atlanta (50 inches/127 centimeters), or many other cities.

How did the Pacific Northwest get its rainy reputation? Because much of the region has more cloudy days and more days with rain, even if the amount of rain on any given day is small.

Seattle averages about 157 days each year with at least a trace of rain, compared with 126 days for Boston and 116 days for Atlanta. And it's much cloudier: Seattle has 228 cloudy days per year, while Boston has 161 and Atlanta has only 146. Seattle is so cloudy because the jet stream carries air from the west. This air has been sitting over the Pacific Ocean, where lots of water **evaporates** and forms clouds.

WHEN DOES IT RAIN?

Another difference between the Pacific Northwest and the rest of the country is WHEN the rain falls. In most of the United States, roughly the same amount of precipitation falls every month. But in the Pacific Northwest, most of the rain falls in the winter. The summers are usually quite dry, with even less rainfall than most of the Desert Southwest. This happens because during the winter the jet stream is strong and veers south to flow over Washington and Oregon, bringing rainy weather with it. In the summer, the jet stream is weaker and flows north over Canada. Southern Europe has similar wet, cloudy winters and warm, dry summers. This is called a **Mediterranean climate**.

Did You Know?

During the last week of July and first week of August, there are many places in western Washington that receive rain only once every 10 years.

WHERE DOES IT RAIN?

The western side of the Olympic Mountains gets up to 140 to 160 inches of rain each year (356 to 406 centimeters). That's more rain than anywhere else in the continental United States. But only 45 miles away (42 kilometers), on the other side of the mountains, only 15 inches of rain falls a year (38 centimeters). Why does the climate change from a rainforest to a desert in such a short distance?

It's because of the mountains. As warm air passes over the Pacific Ocean, it picks up moisture. When the warm, moist air hits the coast, it encounters the mountains, which forces the air up along the slopes. When air rises, it cools. Colder air can hold less water vapor than warmer air. So when the air cools, the water vapor in the air **condenses** into tiny droplets and forms clouds. Have you ever seen clouds covering the tops of mountains? If enough water vapor condenses, it rains.

Then, as the air continues to pass over the mountains and descend, the air warms. The air has lost some of its moisture from raining. And now it can hold more water vapor because it is warmer. So the far side of the mountains has much less rainfall. This area is called a **rain shadow**.

Did You Know?

The Mt. Baker ski area in Washington State set the world record for the most snow in one year. In the winter of 1998/1999, it received 96 feet of snow (29 meters). That's enough snow to cover a nine-story building!

Think About It!

Why do you think the record for the most snow in one year belongs to the state of Washington, and not Alaska? What else is required for a lot of snow to fall besides cold temperatures?

In the Pacific Northwest, there is a rain shadow for the Coast Mountains, the Cascades, and the Rocky Mountains. Because of the mountains, the western part of the Pacific Northwest is much wetter than the eastern part.

CHINOOK WINDS AND THE PINEAPPLE EXPRESS

When air flows over the mountains and down the eastern side, it can become a dry, warm wind. These are called **Chinook winds**, named after the Chinook people, who lived along the Columbia River. The Chinook winds can be quite warm and cause big changes in temperature. A strong Chinook wind can melt a foot of snow in one day.

Loma, Montana

Chinook Wind

WORDS TO KNOW

polar night: when the sun stays below the horizon for 24 hours or more. This can occur only in latitudes above 60 degrees.

midnight sun: when the sun stays over the horizon for 24 hours or more. This can occur only in latitudes above 60 degrees.

Chinook winds were responsible for the largest temperature change in 24 hours in the United States. This occurred in Loma, Montana, on January 15, 1972. The temperature rose from -56 degrees to 49 degrees Fahrenheit (-48 to 9 Celsius). That's a 105-degree difference in one day! Another dramatic example of Chinook winds in action occurred on January 12, 1980, in Great Falls, Montana. Residents there saw the temperature rise an astounding 47 degrees Fahrenheit in just 7 minutes (26 degrees Celsius)!

Sometimes unusually warm, moist air comes to the Pacific Northwest. It's called the Pineapple Express because it starts around Hawaii, where pineapple trees grow. When the Pineapple Express is on its way to the Pacific Northwest, look out—rain is coming, and lots of it!

Did You Know?

There was a UFO craze in 1947 when many people thought they saw flying saucers over the Cascade Mountains. This has happened during other times as well, because when air flows over the mountains it can form clouds that are shaped like disks or saucers.

Did You Know?

The city of Yakutat in southeastern Alaska is the rainiest city in the United States, receiving 160 inches of rain per year on average (407 centimeters). Yakutat actually receives more rain than snow because the nearby Pacific Ocean keeps the temperatures mild most of the year.

ALASKA

You might think that Alaska has just one climate: cold. Overall, it certainly is the coldest state in the United States, but there's still a lot of variation. Alaska can be roughly divided into four regions of different climates.

BRRR! A CITY OF COLD

The city of Barrow, Alaska, is the northernmost city in the United States. In the winter, there are about 65 days when the sun never rises. This is called the **polar night**. In the summer, there are 82 straight days where the sun never drops below the horizon. This is called the **midnight sun**. Barrow, Alaska, has about 4,000 permanent residents. Why do you think people choose to live in Barrow? How do you think they cope with the cold and the polar night?

Southeast and South Central: The southeastern and south central parts of the state, which includes the capital of Juneau, have cool, wet winters, and warm summers. Like all coastal areas, its climate is less extreme than areas farther inland. The current in the Pacific Ocean that runs parallel to the coast of Oregon and Washington, also brings warmer water north to the southern coast of Alaska.

Western: The west coast of Alaska often has high winds and storms from the Pacific. There is plenty of sea-ice in the winter.

Interior: The interior region between the Brooks and Alaska Mountain Ranges is cold and dry. These mountains block air coming in from the oceans. Temperatures can range from 80 degrees Fahrenheit in the summer to -50 degrees Fahrenheit in the winter (27 to -46 degrees Celsius). But because the air is dry, it doesn't get nearly as much snow as warmer areas.

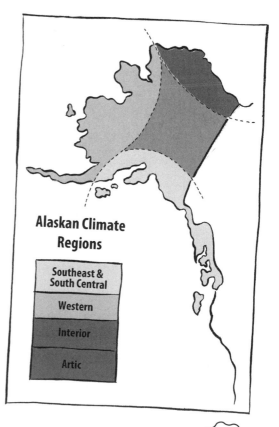

Alaskan Climate Regions

Southeast & South Central

Western

Interior

Artic

Arctic: The far north is cold, but because it borders the Arctic Ocean, it's usually not *quite* as cold as the interior region. Summer is short. Winds blow almost continually.

SKY COLORS

Bright greens, shimmering reds, glowing blues. Have you ever seen these colors in the night sky? Probably not. But you can see them in Alaska or another place in the far north or far south. They're called northern lights, or the **aurora borealis**. In the Southern Hemisphere they are called the aurora australis. These curtains of colored lights can last for just a few minutes or for several hours.

WORDS TO KNOW

aurora borealis: a natural display of shimmering colors in the night sky, usually only seen in the far north. Also called the northern lights.

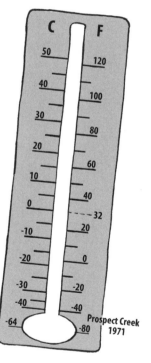

Did You Know?

The lowest temperature recorded in the United States was -80 degrees Fahrenheit (-64 degrees Celsius) in Prospect Creek, Alaska, on January 23, 1971.

The aurora are caused by particles from the sun, called the solar wind. These particles collide with the earth's upper atmosphere. As the particles are absorbed by the atmosphere, gases in the atmosphere emit different colors. Why don't the lights happen all over the earth? Because the particles are drawn toward the magnetism of the North and South Poles.

The northern lights can be seen frequently in the parts of Alaska that are 60 degrees latitude or above. When the sun is especially active, the lights can sometimes even be seen from northern areas of the continental United States.

For a forecast of the strength of the aurora, visit the Geophysical Institute's website: www.gedds.alaska.edu/AuroraForecast/.

MAKE YOUR OWN
RAIN GAUGE

1 Place the ruler inside the container. Use the clear packing tape to tape the ruler against the side of the container, even with the bottom.

2 Place the container in a location that is in the open, and away from trees, your house, or pets. Place heavy objects around the container to keep it from tipping over. You can use the trowel to dig a shallow hole and set the container in the hole.

3 After it rains, measure the rain that fell to the nearest tenth of an inch. Record your measurement in the notebook and empty the rain gauge. Each time it rains in a month, record the rainfall. Add it all up to get a monthly rainfall. Is it what you expected? Does it match the weather service's measurement of monthly rainfall?

SUPPLIES

- clear plastic ruler
- clear plastic or glass container with straight sides and bottom
- clear plastic packing tape
- heavy objects
- trowel
- notebook

Think About It!

Why would simply leaving your rain gauge out for a month not be the best method for measuring monthly rainfall? Think about what might happen to the water during the month, especially on sunny days.

MAKE YOUR OWN
OWN FOG

Make sure to have an adult help with this activity.

1 Fill the jar with hot tap water and let it sit for about a minute. Meanwhile, put several ice cubes into the plastic bag and seal it.

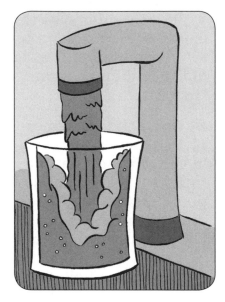

2 Pour out the water from the jar and fill it with hot tap water about 1 or 2 inches deep (2½ to 5 centimeters).

3 With an adult helping you, light the match and blow it out. Lower the match slowly into the jar, letting the smoke fill the jar. Drop the match into the water and quickly place the bag of ice cubes completely over the opening of the jar.

SUPPLIES

- large clear glass or plastic jar
- hot tap water
- ice cubes
- large plastic bag that seals
- match

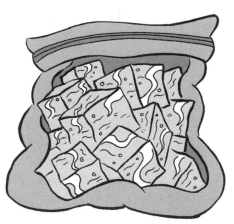

4 Watch the air inside the jar for "fog." Pay particular attention to the area around the ice cubes.

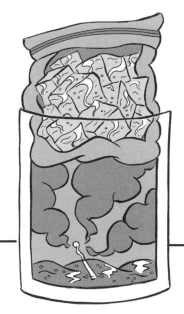

Did You Know?

Cape Disappointment, Washington, is the foggiest place in the continental United States. This is where the Columbia River empties into the Pacific Ocean. There are an average of 106 days each year that are so foggy you can only see a quarter of a mile away or less (a quarter kilometer). Fog often forms here because warm moist air frequently passes over colder ocean water. The cold water cools the air, which then condenses onto salt spray to form fog.

What's Happening?

Fog is like a cloud on the ground. Fog and clouds need three things to form: warm moist air, something that cools the air, and small particles to condense onto. In this experiment, the hot tap water created warm moist air, which was then cooled by the ice. The smoke provided tiny particles for the water vapor to condense onto. In the atmosphere, the tiny particles are dust, smoke, or even salt from sea spray. Did you see wisps of fog coming off the bag of ice into the jar?

CHAPTER 6

RIVERS

Rivers are the lifeblood of a landscape. Plants, animals, and people come together around rivers, and those in the Pacific Northwest are no exception. The rivers in the Pacific Northwest provide water, food, transportation, and recreation. They also **irrigate** crops and **generate** electric power.

The water in rivers comes from precipitation that flows over the surface of the land and into the river. Smaller creeks and streams flow together and form bigger streams and rivers.

Pacific Ocean

WORDS TO KNOW

irrigate: to supply land with water, usually for crops.

generate: to produce energy.

tributary: a stream or river that flows into a larger river.

watershed: the land area that drains into a river or stream.

These smaller streams and rivers are called **tributaries** of the river they flow into. The area of land where all the water eventually flows into a given river is the **watershed** of that river. Rivers flow into the ocean.

There are two major river systems in the Pacific Northwest: the Yukon in Alaska, and the Columbia-Snake River system that runs through Washington, Oregon, Idaho, and western Montana.

THE COLUMBIA-SNAKE RIVER SYSTEM

The Columbia River is fairly steep, which makes it fast and powerful. Beginning at 2,600 feet (792 meters), it drops in elevation twice as much as the Mississippi River in only half the distance. The Columbia empties more water into the Pacific Ocean than any other river in North or South America and is the fourth-largest river in the United States by volume of water.

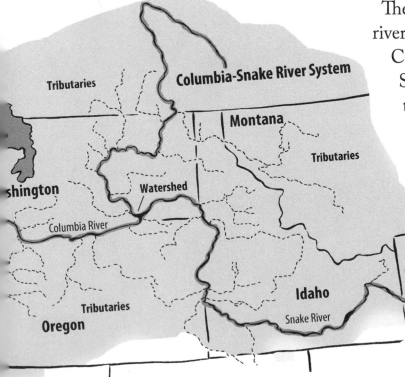

The Columbia starts out as a fast river in the Rocky Mountains of Canada. It enters the United States in Washington and turns sharply west to form the border between Washington and Oregon. Its largest tributary is the Snake River, and the entire system is often called the Columbia-Snake River system.

73

WORDS TO KNOW

gorge: a deep, narrow passage.

portage: to carry boats by land around a waterfall or other impassable part of a river.

subsistence: resources for survival.

species: a group of plants or animals that are related and look like each other.

The Columbia is one of only two rivers that cut through the Cascade Mountains. It does this at the Columbia River Gorge, where the river is often shrouded in fog. The rapids of the **gorge** are too treacherous for boats, so early settlers had to **portage** around the most troublesome spots. Where the Columbia enters the Pacific Ocean, there is a large sandbar that is dangerous for boats. In the last 200 years over 2,000 large ships have sunk here.

SALMON

The rivers of the Pacific Northwest are known for their abundance of salmon. For centuries, native peoples have depended on salmon and other fish for **subsistence**. Different **species** of salmon in the Pacific Northwest include Chinook (also called King), Chum, Coho, Pink, and Sockeye. Today, many people depend on the salmon industry for jobs.

HELLS CANYON

Quick! What's the deepest canyon in the United States? If you said the Grand Canyon, you would be wrong. Measured from the river level to the peak of the highest surrounding mountain, Hells Canyon is the deepest canyon in North America at 7,993 feet (2,436 meters). It is located on the Snake River along the border between Oregon and Idaho.

Salmon live mostly in the ocean, but they **breed** in freshwater. Fish that do this are called **anadromous**. Salmon lay their eggs in mountain streams far from the sea. When the eggs hatch, the tiny salmon stay upstream until they're about a year old. Then they begin their long journey towards the sea. Along the way, their bodies change to make them ready to live in salt water. When they reach the ocean, they travel around for several years, growing much larger.

Sockeye Salmon

WORDS TO KNOW

breed: to produce babies.

anadromous: fish that live mostly in the ocean, but breed in freshwater.

migrate: to move to another environment.

predator: an animal that eats other animals.

Then comes the truly amazing part. When it's time for them to lay their eggs, the salmon **migrate** back to the exact same stream where they hatched! Scientists think the salmon are guided to their hatching grounds by their excellent sense of smell. To get there, they have to fight the current, rocks, waterfalls, **predators**, and human obstacles. Salmon do this without eating during their long journey!

Pink Salmon

75

HOW HYDROELECTRIC ENERGY WORKS

For thousands of years, people have used water wheels to take the energy from flowing water and change it into mechanical energy to do work. Water wheels were often hooked up to huge grinding stones to grind wheat into flour. Hydroelectric power works in a similar way. But it's much more efficient, and it transforms the energy into electricity instead of simply turning a grinding wheel.

Here's how it works:

1. A dam is built across the river to hold back all of the water. This creates a barrier across a river. The water backs up and forms a lake, called a reservoir.

2. The dam funnels the water into a large tunnel, called a penstock.

3. The penstock releases the water at a steady rate into huge turbines. A turbine is like a water wheel on its side, with large blades.

4. The flowing water turns the blades of the turbines. Then the water flows back into the river.

5. The turbine blades are connected to a large metal rod with giant, powerful magnets attached to it. The magnets spin very fast. They are surrounded by large coils of copper wire. When the magnets spin, they create electricity!

The amount of electricity that a hydroelectric plant can produce is determined by two things. One is the volume of water that flows through the turbines. The other is the height that the water falls from. The height from the reservoir to the turbines is called the head. When a lot of water falls from a great height, you can get a lot of electricity.

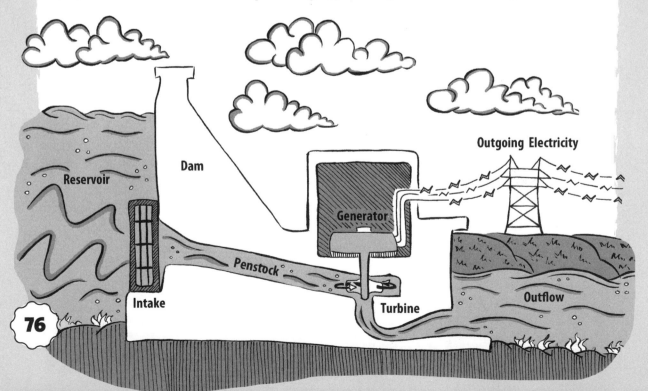

HYDROELECTRIC ENERGY

WORDS TO KNOW

hydroelectric: electricity generated from the energy of flowing water.

renewable resource: any natural resource that isn't used up, that can be replaced.

If you live in Washington or Oregon, chances are that when you turn on the lights in your house, the energy is coming from one of the many rivers in the region. How can water be turned into electricity?

Actually, it isn't the water that is being turned into electricity. It is the energy from the FLOW of the water. A power plant that turns the energy from flowing water into electricity is called a **hydroelectric** plant. Hydro is a Greek word meaning water.

Because the flow of the Columbia River is so strong, it's a good place to make hydroelectric energy. In fact, there are 29 hydroelectric power plants on the Columbia-Snake River system! There are many advantages to hydroelectric energy:

- There's no pollution
- It's a **renewable resource**
- It's inexpensive—often half the cost of other power sources
- It makes it easier to transport goods and people on the river
- It controls flooding
- It allows for irrigation

Did You Know?

The largest concrete structure in North America is the Grand Coulee Dam. It's a mile wide (1½ kilometers) and is located along the Columbia River in western Washington. The Grand Coulee Dam is the largest producer of hydroelectric power in North America and the fifth-largest in the world.

But there are also major problems with dams. By slowing a river down, a dam causes it to flow at a relatively steady rate. But that means sediments don't get carried downstream the same way and they end up clogging the river.

swim bladder: an air-filled sac that many fish have to help them stay afloat.

The much bigger problem with dams, though, is their impact on the salmon population. For every one salmon today, there used to be 100 salmon. There are a few reasons for this. One is that the pressure from the dams can burst the **swim bladders** in the fish, killing them. Another is that the dams form a barrier for the salmon when they're trying to migrate. Finally, the hydroelectric plants increase the temperature of the water. Salmon are sensitive to water temperature, especially when young.

One thing that can help the salmon is a fish ladder. This is a channel built around a dam that gradually rises from the water level below the dam to the water level above it. Fish are funneled toward the ladder so they can make their way up and around the dam. Then they can continue their swim upstream.

ELWHA RIVER RESTORATION

The Elwha River flows through Olympic National Park in Washington. It has two dams on it and both are set to be removed beginning in September 2011. The removal of the dams will restore the river to its free-flowing state, sometimes called a "wild" river. These will be the largest dams removed to date in the United States.

The Elwha River was one of the few in the Pacific Northwest to contain all five species of Pacific Salmon. But when the dams were built, in 1910 and 1923, they didn't have any fish ladders, so fish were blocked from traveling upstream. Before the dams were built, it was estimated there were about 392,000 wild salmon. Now there are only about 3,000.

By the 1980s, people saw that the dams blocked or killed fish, and lots of sediment had built up behind the dams. In 1992, Congress passed an act to have the dams removed. After the dams are removed, the salmon will be able to swim up the river the way they used to.

Did You Know?

Some salmon migrate up rivers as far as 700 miles from the sea (1,127 kilometers)! They can travel an average of 34 miles per day (55 kilometers). The largest King salmon in the world was caught on the Kenai River in southern Alaska. It weighed nearly 100 pounds (45 kilograms)!

King Salmon

79

WORDS TO KNOW

wetlands: an area where the land is soaked with water. Wetlands are often important habitats for fish, plants, and wildlife.

Where salmon and trout go, bears and eagles will follow. As the fish return upstream to all 70 miles of the river (113 kilometers), the entire ecosystem will be restored. And as the sediment is allowed to flow downstream, it will create beaches and **wetlands** where the river flows into the ocean.

Chinook Salmon

YUKON RIVER

The Yukon is a remote and beautiful river that stretches for 1,982 miles across the interior of Alaska (3,190 kilometers). There are vast wetlands where the Yukon approaches the ocean. These marshes spread out for hundreds of miles and are home to a huge number of birds and other animals. The watershed of the Yukon River is larger than the state of Texas. Even though it's a very long river, the Yukon only has four bridges large enough for a vehicle to cross. The Yukon discharges more than 200,000 cubic feet of water per second at its mouth (5,663 cubic meters). And each year it carries more than 60 million tons of sediment (54 million metric tons) into the ocean that has been eroded from the mountains. That's as much as about 3 million big dump trucks can hold!

Think About It!

Do you think hydroelectric power plants and their dams should be removed from the rivers in the Pacific Northwest? What factors might affect your opinion about a specific dam?

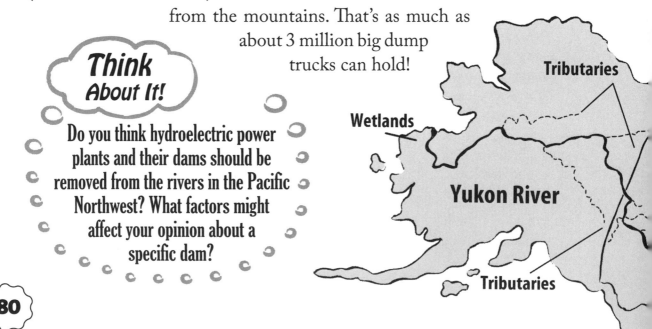

Tributaries

Wetlands

Yukon River

Tributaries

GOLDRUSH!

In 1896 a huge strike of gold was discovered on the Klondike River, which is a tributary of the Yukon. The Klondike strike triggered the biggest gold rush in the world. People came from all over the world to try to find gold, traveling up the Yukon to get to the gold strike. A few became very rich, but most suffered from cold and lack of food.

TRANSPORTATION

For centuries, the Columbia and Yukon Rivers have been important transportation routes in the Pacific Northwest. Native peoples used both rivers as ways to get from place to place. In modern times, huge barges carry large amounts of wheat, barley, paper, minerals, and cars along the rivers.

Barges are much more efficient at carrying large loads than trucks or even trains. They require only one third as much fuel as a truck per ton of goods carried. One barge can carry 3,500 tons or more (3,175 metric tons). It would take 134 large trucks to carry all that!

Did You Know?

Multnomah Falls is on the Oregon side of the Columbia River in the Columbia River Gorge. It is the second-highest, year-round waterfall in the United States, at 620 feet high (189 meters).

For a long time, the Yukon River was the only means of travel in the Alaskan interior. Around World War II, the Alaska Highway was built, which linked Alaska with the rest of the United States. Later, a network of roads was built connecting villages, and the Yukon was no longer used as much for travel.

MAKE YOUR OWN
WATER WHEEL

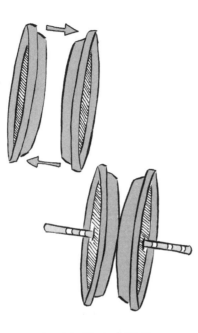

SUPPLIES

- 2 disposable plastic plates
- pencil
- 12 small, bathroom-size plastic cups
- stapler
- drinking straw
- scissors
- string
- water hose with a sprayer connected to a spigot
- tape
- pennies

1 Put the 2 plates together. Balance the plates on the eraser end of the pencil to find the exact center, and mark the center. Then flip the plates over so they're back to back. Have an adult help you push the pencil through the middle of both.

2 Ease the two plates apart so there's about an inch between them (2½ centimeters). Staple the cups between the plates with the cups on their side, all facing in the same direction. Most of each cup should be sticking out. Leave about an inch of space between the cups. Depending on the size of your cups and plates, you may not need all of the cups.

3 Pull out the pencil and push the straw through the hole. Cut a long piece of string and pull it through the straw.

4 Find a place outside that can get wet and tie your water wheel between two points, like the branches of a tree. The spot you choose should be near your hose. Get permission from an adult, then use the hose to spray water at the cups in a narrow stream. Watch the wheel turn.

5 Make your water wheel work for you by attaching a bucket to lift things. To do this, take another plastic cup and cut two holes opposite each other near the top. Cut a short piece of string and loop it through the holes to make a handle. Cut another string a bit shorter than your water wheel is above the ground. Tie one end to the straw and fasten with tape. Tie the other end to your cup's handle.

6 Place a penny in your cup and see if your water wheel can lift the cup when you spray it with water. Try different numbers of pennies: how much can your water wheel lift? Can you think of any way to make the wheel lift your cup of pennies faster? *(Hint: What would happen if you could change the thickness of the straw?)*

Did You Know?

Water wheels were used around 6,000 years ago in Greece to grind corn. In the 1700s, water wheels were used for grinding grains into flour and pumping water. Water wheels were first used to generate electricity in 1880 at the Wolverine Chair Factory in Grand Rapids, Michigan.

MAKE YOUR OWN
RIVER BED

1 Select an area outside for the experiment and get an adult's approval for the location. The area will have water draining onto it, and possibly some spillage of sand. Ideally, the area is within reach of a hose connected to a water spigot.

2 Place the box on the board. Raise one end of the board onto a brick. Make a V-shaped cut into the cardboard at the lower end so that the bottom of the "V" is about 2 inches from the bottom of the box (5 centimeters).

3 Cut the garbage bag open and line the box with the bag. Push the plastic down into the V-shaped notch. Using the trowel, fill the plastic-lined box with sand or dirt. The dirt should be about 3 inches deep (7½ centimeters) at the upper end, tapering down to about 1 inch deep (2½ centimeters) at the lower end.

4 Use the trowel to make an S-shaped groove in the dirt about 1 inch deep. The groove should start at the top and end at the notch with one curve to the left and one to the right. The groove represents a river channel.

5 Place the hose at the higher end of the channel and turn the water on to a trickle. If you are using a pitcher of water, slowly pour the water into the channel at the higher end. After a short time, the water will drain out at the bottom through the V-shaped notch that you cut.

6 Watch the channel over the next few minutes. Does the shape of the channel change? Is sand or dirt carried downstream? After awhile, turn the water off, smooth out the dirt, and try making your stream in different ways.

continues on next page . . .

7 You can place your stream table at a higher slope by propping it up on two bricks. You can vary the flow of water coming from the hose. Start with different shapes to your channel, or start with no channel at all. Try filling the channel with pebbles about halfway down the slope. What happens to the water?

What's Happening?

The volume of water and the slope of a river are important factors for the shape a river takes, and how much sediment it carries downstream. The greater the slope, like when you raised the board onto two bricks, the more sediment a river will transport downstream.

Meandering rivers are rivers that have an "S" shape. They form where it's relatively flat. The meanders, or curves, grow outward with time. This is because the water on the inside of the curve travels more slowly than water on the outside. So there's more erosion on the outside of the curve. This makes the curve bigger and bigger over time.

CHAPTER 7

ECOSYSTEMS

What could be more different than a lush rainforest bursting with life and huge trees, and the **tundra**, a land of extreme cold where trees don't even have a chance to grow? Both ecosystems can be found in the Pacific Northwest, and each is beautiful and important in its own unique way.

WORDS TO KNOW

tundra: a plain in the far north where the soil below the surface is permanently frozen.

An ecosystem is all the plants and animals that live in a place. It is also the physical environment itself—the soil, air, water, and even the sunlight.

WORDS TO KNOW

temperate rainforest: a forest in the temperate zone, halfway between the equator and the poles, that receives high rainfall.

organism: a living thing, such as a plant or animal.

mammals: a class of animals that includes humans. Mammals have backbones and nourish their young with milk.

epiphyte: a plant that lives on another plant. It gets its food and moisture directly from the air.

lichens: organisms that are part fungi and part algae.

biomass: the total mass of living things, both alive and recently living.

nutrients: the substances in food and soil that keep animals and plants healthy and growing.

Think About It!

In the rainforest, the largest **organisms** are the trees. In the tundra, **mammals** are the largest organisms.

Everything in an ecosystem interacts with each other. The plants need the soil and sunlight, the animals eat the plants, and the plants also depend on the animals.

TEMPERATE RAINFOREST

When you think of a rainforest, you probably imagine the Amazon Rainforest in South America. Something hot and humid with huge, broad-leaf trees, and exotic animals like monkeys, toucan birds, and piranha fish.

Most people don't realize that North America has a rainforest too, but it's a **temperate rainforest**. This rainforest runs right along the coast of the Pacific Ocean from southeastern Alaska to Oregon. Some people also include the forests of northern California in this temperate rainforest. Unlike tropical rainforests, temperate rainforests are far away from the equator. They are much cooler and have quite different plants and animals.

What are some of the characteristics of the rainforest in the Pacific Northwest?

- Rain! Rain! Rain! The Pacific Northwest rainforest receives between 140 and 167 inches each year—that's 12 to 14 feet (3½ to 4 meters)!

- Lots of fog.

- Lots of **epiphytes**, such as ferns, mosses, and **lichens**.

- A tempcrate latitude, between the Arctic Circle and the equator.

- A mean annual temperature between 39 and 54 degrees Fahrenheit (4 and 12 degrees Celsius).

- Proximity to the ocean, with mountains on the other (eastern) side to block extreme weather.

- The highest levels of **biomass** of any area on earth. Although tropical rainforests have more species of plants and animals, the temperate rainforest has more biomass. Biomass is the total mass of living and recently living organisms, including wood, leaf litter, moss, other living plants, and soil.

EPI-WHATS?

Epiphytes live on other plants and are sometimes called "air plants" because they get their **nutrients** and moisture directly from the air and rain. Since epiphytes have to absorb water directly from the rain as it falls and from the air, they like to live in moist environments. In the Pacific Northwest rainforest, the epiphytes are mainly ferns, mosses, and lichens. They cover branches and tree trunks, spreading a green blanket over the forest.

ALASKAN RAINFOREST

More than one quarter of the world's coastal temperate rainforests are in southeast Alaska. The mountains come very close to the sea, so the rainforest goes only a little way inland. But where there are **fjords**, or inlets, the rainforest goes in and wraps around them. There are thousands of islands in the Alaskan rainforest. Black bears, eagles, and salmon fill the land, air, and sea.

OLYMPIC NATIONAL PARK

Perhaps the best example of a rainforest in the lower 48 states is at Olympic National Park in Washington state. Founded in 1909 to protect the elk and the ancient forest, the park has three rainforests along four rivers. The rainforests grow close to the coast on the west side of the mountains along the river valleys. The park rainforests contain:

WORDS TO KNOW

fjord: a narrow, deep inlet of the sea with steep slopes on both sides.

fungi: a division of organisms including yeasts, molds, and mushrooms.

mycelium: the body of a fungus that is composed of many branching, threadlike filaments.

decompose: to break down, or rot, into simpler parts.

photosynthesis: the process where plants use sunlight and water to make their own food.

- Eight species of ferns.

- 500-year-old trees that are over 200 feet tall (61 meters). The tallest trees are Douglas firs and hemlocks.

- Rivers that are fed by glaciers. Their milky blue color is because glaciers grind up rocks into what is called "glacial flour."

- Mammals, including the Roosevelt elk, black bears, marmots, bats, and river otters.

- Birds, including woodpeckers and endangered species of marbled murrelets and spotted owls.

FUNGI!

Fungi include mold, yeasts, and mushrooms. They are not plants or animals. Fungi grow and build networks that look a bit like a cobweb, called a **mycelium**. The mycelium will sometimes produce "fruit." An example of fungi fruit is a mushroom.

Fungi play an important role in the rainforest ecosystem. They are able to break down wood and other plant material. Without fungi, dead trees and plants wouldn't **decompose**. They would just pile up into a big mess.

Fungi often look like shelves growing out of trees. This tough, woody fungus is called bracket fungus. It can grow to 3 feet across (1 meter) and live as long as 50 years. Bracket fungi work to break down wood on dead trees that are still standing.

Fungi can also help trees live. Many evergreen trees are partners with fungi. The fungi attach to the root tips underground and help deliver nutrients to the tree. They also kill harmful bacteria. In return, the tree gives the fungi sugar from **photosynthesis**. This relationship is especially important in a tree's first few years when it has a harder time getting enough nutrients.

Bracket Fungi

Did You Know?

A colony of honey mushrooms in Malheur National Forest in eastern Oregon is considered by many to be the world's largest organism by area. On the surface, the mushrooms look like separate organisms, but they are all connected underneath. The colony is thought to be about 8,000 years old and covers over 2,224 acres (900 hectares) of forested land. That's as big as 2,000 football fields!

NURSE LOGS

Dead wood is dead, right? Not exactly. True, the tree itself is no longer alive, but if you look closely at a dead tree, you'll see lots of life. Usually, dead trees remain standing for awhile and are called snags. They make great homes for owls and other birds and animals. Eventually they fall to the ground, where they are called nurse logs, because they nurse along tiny seedling trees and give them a head start on life.

Rotting trees lying on the ground are moist and covered with moss. They're full of water, leaves, and soil. And there's more sunlight here because of the gap overhead where the tree used to stand. It's the perfect place for tiny tree seedlings to sprout and grow.

You can often tell where a nurse log used to be because there's now a line of trees with their roots above ground—the trees look like they're on stilts. As the trees grew, their roots spread over the log and down to the ground. After the nurse log completely rotted away, the trees were left standing in a line.

Did You Know?

Ninety-six percent of big spruce and hemlock trees got their start on a nurse log. Only about one seed in 10,000 becomes a large tree.

THE TUNDRA

WORDS TO KNOW

permafrost: the ground underneath the top layer of soil that is permanently frozen.

The tundra is a land of extreme cold. In the United States, the tundra is found along the northern and western coasts of Alaska. It might seem like there would be no life on the tundra, but there's plenty of it—it's just a little harder to find than in a rainforest.

The tundra is so cold that trees cannot grow on it. That's because the ground is permanently frozen just under the topsoil. This frozen ground is called **permafrost**—it doesn't thaw, even in the summer. Plants can grow on the tundra, but they must have shallow roots. They also have to grow low to the ground because of icy winds there. The main plants are lichens, mosses, and grasses.

SUMMER ON THE TUNDRA

In the summer, the sun never sets. The snow and ice melt, but not the permafrost. Because the ground underneath is still frozen, the melted water doesn't have anywhere to drain. So a lot of the tundra turns into cold marshes and pools of water. The summers are short and cool in the tundra, averaging about 50 degrees Fahrenheit (10 degrees Celsius).

But it's warm enough for plants and animals to pack a lot of activity into those short months—mainly July and August. Plants burst into bloom. Animals breed and raise their young. There are also lots of mosquitoes, flies, bees, and butterflies flying around.

Did You Know?

Lichens are organisms that are part fungi and part algae. The two parts help each other survive. The fungi provide water and shelter to the algae. Since the algae are a green plant they can use photosynthesis to make their own food, which they share with the fungi.

Because there are so many insects, birds migrate up from the south to eat them. The constant daylight allows them longer times to eat and feed their young. Geese, swans, ducks, sandpipers, and plovers all come to the tundra in the summer.

WINTER ON THE TUNDRA

How do all of those plants and animals survive in the winter? The sun never rises, and temperatures average about -22 degrees Fahrenheit (-30 degrees Celsius). Animals and birds, of course, can move. Many of them migrate to warmer climates during the winter.

MAKE YOUR OWN FUNGI

SUPPLIES

- wooden board a few feet long (1 meter), and at least a foot wide (30 centimeters)
- pile of leaves
- magnifying glass

1 Place the board under a tree on top of fallen leaves. Let your family know what you're doing so no one disturbs the board.

2 After four to six weeks, turn the board over and examine the underside. Look at it with the magnifying glass. Do you see thin filaments that look like a spider's web? These are the mycelia of fungi. You may also see little nodules. These are tiny fruiting bodies. Mushrooms are examples of fruiting bodies on other types of fungi.

Did You Know?

Lichens are an important food source for animals such as caribou, especially in the winter. They grow on rocks or in thick mats and are often beautiful colors of red, green, and yellow.

The Arctic tern is a bird that migrates between the Arctic Circle in the north and Antarctica in the south. That means it travels over 24,000 miles each year in search of food (38,624 kilometers)! It experiences night for only a few months each year during its flight over the temperate regions of the earth. As a result, the Arctic Tern experiences more sunlight than any other living creature.

Other animals stay and have their own ways of adapting. Lemmings, which are small mammals, burrow beneath the snow so they are protected from the wind. The snow insulates them from the extreme cold, and hides them from predators. The arctic fox grows two layers of extremely dense fur. In the summer its fur is brown and white, but in the winter it turns all white for camouflage.

Think About It!

The tundra is an extremely harsh and difficult place to live. What about where you live? What is easy or difficult about your own "habitat"?

MAKE YOUR OWN
TERRARIUM

1 Wash the soda bottles, remove the labels, and dry them. With help from an adult, cut the top off of one bottle, and cut the other bottle in half. Using two bottles allows you to make a taller terrarium.

2 Place pebbles on the bottom of the taller bottle to a depth of a couple of inches (5 centimeters). The pebbles will allow water to settle in the bottom so the soil doesn't get too muddy. If you have activated charcoal, place about half an inch on top of the pebbles (1 centimeter). The activated charcoal helps to purify the water and keep the terrarium clean. If you have sphagnum moss, place a layer on top of the charcoal. The moss keeps the soil from settling into the charcoal. Finally, put at least 2 inches of potting soil on top (5 centimeters).

SUPPLIES

- two clear, 2-liter soda bottles—one must have the top still on
- scissors
- pebbles
- activated charcoal (optional), available at pet stores
- sphagnum moss (optional)
- potting soil
- seeds, or 2 to 3 small plants that like moisture, like small ferns
- pretty rocks
- water

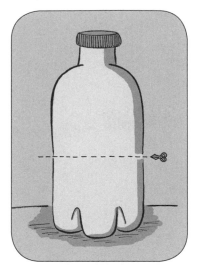

3 If you have seeds, plant the seeds to the depth noted on the seed package. If you have plants in pots, take the plants out of the pots and loosen the roots. Then dig a small hole in the soil and place the plant in the hole. Pat the soil around your plants or seeds. You can add pretty rocks or small sculptures as decoration.

4 Gently pour water on the soil until it is damp. A small amount of water should settle in the pebbles. Take the top half of the bottle that you cut in half and slide it over the bottom half of the bottle containing the soil. The bottles should overlap about an inch (2½ centimeters). If you have difficulty sliding the pieces over each other, make small cuts in one part. Make sure the bottle cap is on the top.

5 Place your terrarium near a window, but not so that the sun shines directly on it. You can put the terrarium in the sun for an hour or so, but it will heat up too much if you leave it there for a long time. Every week or so, check your terrarium. The inside of the top should look misty, but not covered in water droplets.

continues on next page . . .

6 Take off the top and feel the soil. Is it dry? If so, add some water. If the inside of the bottle is covered in beads of water or the soil is soaked, keep the top off for an hour or so until the terrarium dries out a bit. If any plants are yellowed or a bit too large, gently trim them before putting the top back on. If a plant seems to be sickly or is very large, replace it with another plant.

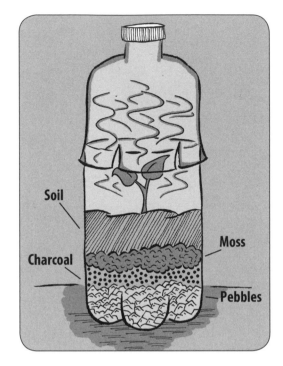

What's Happening?

A terrarium is a small garden that is grown inside a covered container. As the water is heated, it evaporates and becomes water vapor, which is a gas. Because the container is closed, the water vapor condenses onto the sides of the container. This condensation then "rains" onto the plants below, watering them. It's a continual closed-loop process that acts a little bit like a rainforest ecosystem.

MAKE YOUR OWN
SORTING TRICK

1 Fill the jar almost to the top with sand. Put several pieces of gravel or pebbles on top so that they just touch the lid, and are surrounded by sand.

2 Challenge a friend or parent to move the gravel to the other end of the jar without opening the lid. Let them try for a while, then tell them it needs a special touch.

3 Turn the jar upside down and lightly bang it on the table over and over. If you want, you can say some magic words. The gravel will slowly rise. When it gets to the top, simply turn the jar back over.

SUPPLIES

- narrow, transparent jar with a lid
- sand
- gravel or pebbles

What's Happening?

Even though the gravel might be denser than the sand, when you bang the jar against the table, the sand flows around the gravel and settles underneath it, forcing the gravel upward. A similar process happens in very cold regions like the tundra. The repeated freezing and thawing of groundwater pushes rocks toward the surface as dirt and pebbles settle underneath the larger rocks. When they get to the surface, the rocks form what is called "patterned ground." These patterns can be circles, polygons, or stripes. It looks like a human artist arranged the stones, but it's really the freeze-thaw cycle at work.

CHAPTER 8

THE COAST

The coast is where land and water meet, and it is an interesting place. The people, plants, and animals of the Pacific Northwest interact in complicated ways with the ocean beyond.

All oceans have currents, which are continuous, directed movements of water over hundreds and thousands of miles. The current in the North Pacific moves in a clockwise direction. As the water heads east, it branches as it gets close to North America—one branch heads north and the other south.

WORDS TO KNOW

upwelling: when colder, denser, nutrient-rich water rises to the ocean's surface because the surface water has been diverted by wind.

phytoplankton: microscopic algae, usually single-celled, that drift on the current.

microscopic: so tiny that you need a microscope to see them.

The water off southern Alaska is warmer than expected because it's coming from the south. Meanwhile, the water off Washington and Oregon is colder because it's coming from the north. Ocean temperatures affect the climate of an area, which helps to explain why the weather on the southern coast of Alaska is warmer than you might think it would be.

Upwelling is another reason that the water is colder along the western coast of the United States. This happens when the wind pushes the surface water south and west—away from the land. To replace this lost surface water, deeper water rises, or upwells, from down below. Deeper water is colder water.

Colder water also has a lot more nutrients than warmer water. These nutrients are used by **phytoplankton**, which are **microscopic** plants that fish love to eat. So it should be no surprise that half of the world's fisheries can be found in areas where upwelling happens—such as in the Pacific Northwest.

Pacific Currents

PLANKTON

We twirl and swirl,
We float and drift.
In getting around,
We're not too swift.
Which makes us prey
For the anemone
And whales and fish and …
The whole dang sea.
They gobble and gulp us;
We're an easy mark.

And if they should miss,
We sink to the dark.
Now tell us straight.

What would you choose?
The belly of a whale,
Or a diatom ooze?

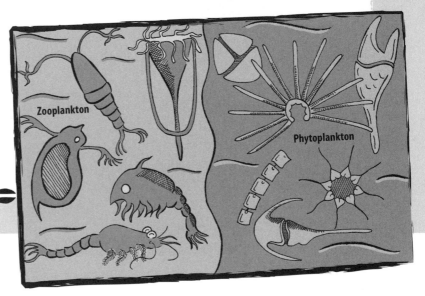

Zooplankton

Phytoplankton

HOW LONG IS THE COAST?

Alaska has a coastline that's 33,000 miles in length (53,108 kilometers), including islands. That's longer than the entire coastline of the continental United States. It's about 6,600 miles (10,622 kilometers) without islands. The coasts of Washington and Oregon are also long, because they have lots of inlets and variations.

But what does it mean to say a coastline is a certain length? In truth, a coastline doesn't actually have a set length. That's because it depends on how you measure it. Think about a beach. Do you just measure it as a straight line? What about if there's a small inlet—do you measure around that area? If you do, the length of the coastline will be greater.

What about a small tide pool—do you measure around that? Coastlines are complex at all scales, even at very small scales.

The Pacific Northwest has one of the most complex coastlines in the world. That makes it an interesting place and an inviting one for many animals. If you were a small animal trying to hide from a predator, where would you rather live—on a long, straight beach or on a beach with lots of coves, inlets, rocks, and tide pools?

ENERGY FROM THE SEA

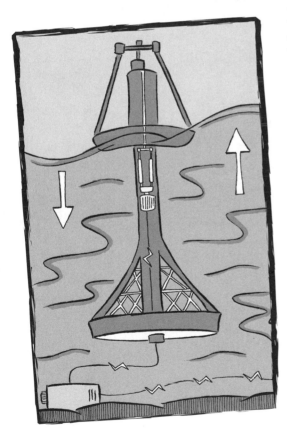

Have you ever played in ocean waves? If so, you know that waves have a lot of energy. They pound the beaches every single day, all day, along virtually every beach in the world. Scientists estimate that using only a tiny percentage of all that energy could supply enough power for the whole world.

Of course, the trick is how to capture the ocean's natural energy. One possible way is being tried at Reedsport, Oregon. A wave energy park is being developed there, using buoys. As the waves pass the buoys, the buoys are lifted up and down in a circular pattern. This movement is converted to electricity. The project is expected to produce enough power for 1,000 homes.

THE FOOD WEB

Would you believe that the largest animals in the ocean, including whales and sharks, depend on tiny, single-celled plants? These phytoplankton are too small to see with the naked eye. They drift with the current and use photosynthesis and the energy from the sun to make their own "food." Phytoplankton are eaten by microscopic animals called zooplankton. Other larger animals then eat the zooplankton. The plants and animals are often connected in complicated ways. Altogether, these connections are called the **food web**.

The Pacific Northwest has lots of phytoplankton because they grow well in the cold, upwelling water. The next time you eat salmon or tuna, thank a phytoplankton!

Pacific Food Web

Orca

Fish & Crabs

Anemones & Barnacles

Zooplankton

Phytoplankton

WORDS TO KNOW

food web: a complex set of feeding relationships between plants and animals.

kelp: large seaweed, which is a form of algae.

ALGAL BLOOMS

Small things can sometimes cause big problems. Sometimes, phytoplankton multiply to huge numbers. This is called an algal bloom. Algal blooms can cover a large area—sometimes even hundreds of miles!

Some algae produce toxic chemicals, and when these bloom it is called a harmful algal bloom. Within hours, a harmful algal bloom can kill hundreds or even thousands of fish, seabirds, turtles, and mammals. The causes of harmful algal blooms are unclear, but scientists are able to monitor the blooms so that fisheries can be closed when they happen.

Algal Blooms

KELP FORESTS

Kelp forests are incredible underwater wonderlands. From above the surface of the water, they look like brown mats. But underwater, the kelp are huge seaweeds up to 100 feet in length (30 meters), waving back and forth in the water. Their movement can be gentle and serene, or swirling and even violent during storms. A kelp forest has a greenish light from the kelp itself and the phytoplankton that live there.

Did You Know?

There's algae in your ice cream! Kelp is harvested for a gel called algin. Algin is used in cosmetics, clothing, toothpaste, and food such as ice cream. Look at food labels for ingredients such as algin, alginic acid, nori, or carageenan. They're all forms of kelp.

Kelp Forest

Giant Kelp

Sea Otter

Blue Rockfish

Anemone   Purple Urchin

Ochre Sea Star

Kelp forests can be found all along the coasts of Washington, Oregon, and Alaska.

Kelp love the West Coast because of its rocky surfaces that allow the kelp to attach to the bottom. They also love the cool, nutrient-rich waters caused by the upwelling along the coast. Like plants, kelp use photosynthesis and the energy from the sun to make their own food, so they can only live in relatively shallow water. Under the right conditions, kelp can grow more than a foot in a single day (⅓ meter)!

Kelp forests are home to an incredible variety of sea life—more than almost any other ocean community. Kelp forests are much like forests on land, providing shade, cover, and food for plants and animals. Sea stars, worms, sponges, urchins, anemones, and sea cucumbers live at the base of these forests. Farther up, you can find shrimp, octopus, and all types of fish. Predators such as larger fish, eel, and sea otters can also be found visiting kelp forests.

RAZORBACK CLAMS

People along the coast of the Pacific Northwest have long traditions of harvesting razorback clams. In the 1980s, 13 million razor clams were harvested each year. To harvest clams, you just use a shovel or rake to dig down in the sand at low tide. Nowadays, the fisheries set limits on how many clams each person can harvest so that the clam population does not decline. Today, about 2 or 3 million clams are harvested each year.

MARINE MAMMALS

When you think of the ocean, you don't usually think of mammals. After all, mammals breathe air, not water. The ocean can be cold, dark, and filled with predators. But mammals have adapted in many ways, and they're an important part of the Pacific Northwest waters.

There are three main groups of **marine** mammals in the Pacific Northwest: **cetaceans** (including whales, dolphins, and porpoises), sea otters, and **pinnipeds** (including walruses, seals, and sea lions). All of them have bodies that are streamlined to make it easier to move through the water. They also have special ways to stay warm, communicate, and catch their food.

WORDS TO KNOW

marine: found in the ocean.

cetaceans: marine mammals that are nearly hairless with flippers and a flat notched tail, such as whales, dolphins, and porpoises.

pinnipeds: marine mammals that are fin-footed and include walruses, seals, and sea lions.

WORDS TO KNOW

extinction: when a group of plants or animals dies out and there are no more left in the world.

sanctuary: a place where wildlife is protected.

Many of theses mammals were hunted almost to **extinction** in the last century. All hunting of marine mammals was banned in the United States in 1972, and **sanctuaries** have been established to help protect their habitat. Most marine mammals have recovered somewhat, but they still need our help to have healthy populations.

FOCUS ON CETACEANS: ORCAS

The orca is a highly intelligent toothed whale. Three pods, or groups, of orca spend the summer and fall around the San Juan Islands in Washington's Puget Sound. The same animals come back each year.

Orcas hunt together, much like wolves. Their complex communication includes a series of clicks and squeaks to share information with each other. Each pod has its own set of calls, which the young learn from their mothers. When they're hunting salmon, the Puget Sound orcas use a series of clicks that fish can't hear. But when orcas are hunting mammals, they avoid using clicks because mammals have excellent hearing.

Think About It!

Different groups of people have their own sounds and words to communicate, just like the different pods of orcas.

FOCUS ON SEA OTTERS

Sea otters are fun to watch as they roll around in the water and play. They don't seem to have a care in the world! Most of the world's sea otters live in coastal Alaska, but a few also live in coastal Washington. Sea otters are one of the few mammals to use tools—they use rocks to break open clams and other mollusks.

Groups of whales, walruses, seals, and sea lions are called pods. A group of sea otters is called a raft.

Sea otters are about 4 feet long (1⅓ meters) with a small round head and two layers of thick fur. Their diet consists of fish, mollusks, and crabs. They eat while floating on their back, using their tummy as a table! And they eat a lot: about one third of their weight every day. That's because they have to burn a lot of energy to stay warm.

Hair keeps them warm too. Sea otters have about one million hairs per inch on their body—that's more hair in an inch than you have on your entire head! They constantly groom their fur by licking it and blowing into it. Oil spills are deadly for sea otters because the oil mats their fur. Matted fur can't keep them warm.

Did You Know?

One of the largest gatherings of walruses in the world typically occurs on Round Island off the southwestern coast of Alaska. There have been up to 14,000 walruses counted in one day. Some of the male walruses weigh almost 4,000 pounds (1,814 kilograms)!

FOCUS ON PINNIPEDS: WALRUSES

Walruses are huge marine mammals. A single walrus can weigh 2 to 3 tons (1.81 to 2.72 metric tons)—more than the average car!

Try touching your canine teeth (the ones that are slightly pointed). Now imagine if these teeth were 3 feet long (1 meter). That's what walruses have—3-foot-long canine teeth called tusks. It helps them make holes in the ice and helps them climb out of the water onto the ice. Males also fight using their tusks. Walruses have a layer of fat, called blubber, that's up to 6 inches thick (15 centimeters). The blubber keeps them warm.

MAKE YOUR OWN
COASTLINE DRAWING

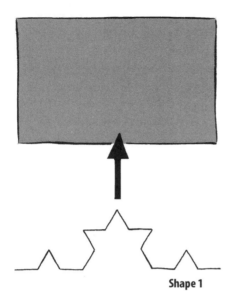

Shape 1

1 On the first sheet of paper, use the black marker and the ruler to draw Shape 1 as large as will fit on the paper.

2 Place the second sheet of paper on top of the first and lightly trace the shape from the first paper using the pencil. Then using the marker, add in the details so the shape looks like Shape 2. You don't have to use the ruler or be exact. Just get the general shape.

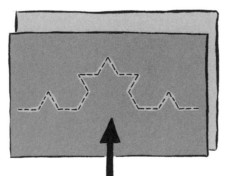

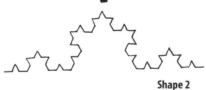

Shape 2

SUPPLIES

- 3 sheets of notebook paper
- black marker
- ruler
- pencil

3 Repeat step 2, except trace the drawing from the second paper, and add in details to look like Shape 3. Again, you don't need to be exact.

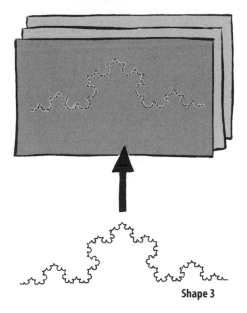

4 Measure the length of the lines on each of the three papers. Which is the longest?

Shape 3

What's Happening?

This is an example of a fractal, which is a shape that is repeated at smaller and smaller scales. Parts of the shape are similar to the whole shape. If you look at your drawing, you'll see that the shape of a small part of it is like the shape of the whole thing. You could keep making this shape more and more complex at smaller and smaller scales. The only limit would be the thickness of your pencil. Although a coastline isn't an exact fractal, it has many of the same characteristics. Saying exactly how long a coastline is can be a tricky matter!

See if you can find examples of fractals in your everyday life. Can you find a leaf where parts of the leaf have a similar shape to the whole leaf? Can you find any self-similar patterns in branches, roots, rain, snow, or ice?

PUGET SOUND

Puget Sound is a huge inlet in Washington. On a map, it looks like an arm of the ocean reaching into the land. This arm touches the state's capital, Olympia, as well as its largest city, Seattle.

WORDS TO KNOW

estuary: a protected area where saltwater and freshwater mix together.

eelgrass: a marine plant with long narrow leaves that grows in estuaries. Eelgrass supports a diverse habitat.

Why were these major cities built on Puget Sound? Because it connects to the ocean, but is also protected from violent ocean storms. That means that large freighters can transport goods to and from the many cities along the coast. Puget Sound has seven major ports.

Puget Sound also has lots of freshwater entering it from the Cascade Mountain and Olympic Mountain watersheds. Areas where saltwater and freshwater mix together and are protected from ocean waves are called **estuaries**. Estuaries are usually full of nutrients, so they're often home to a large variety of plants and animals.

In particular, Puget Sound has lots of kelp—and over 40 square miles of **eelgrass** (105 square kilometers). Like kelp, eelgrass grows in shallow water and provides food and shelter for lots of different animals. You'll find orcas, gray whales, seals, sea lions, salmon, and numerous species of birds in Puget Sound. Like all of the Pacific Northwest, Puget Sound is a complex, beautiful place!

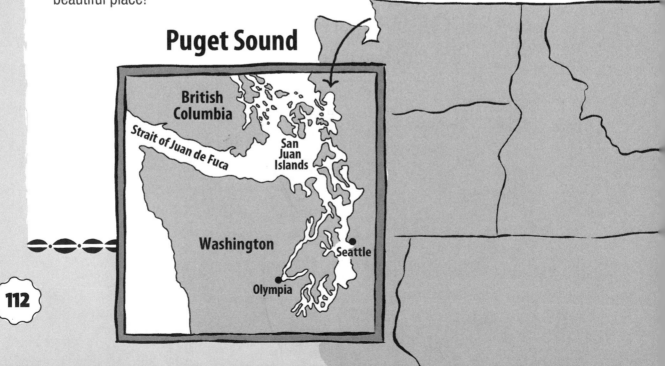

Puget Sound

British Columbia

Strait of Juan de Fuca

San Juan Islands

Washington

Seattle

Olympia

algae: plants that live mainly in water. They do not have leaves, roots, or stems.

anadromous: fish that live mostly in the ocean, but breed in freshwater.

asthenosphere: the semi-molten middle layer of the earth that includes the lower mantle. Much of the asthenosphere flows slowly, like Silly Putty.

atmosphere: the air surrounding the earth.

aurora borealis: a natural display of shimmering colors in the night sky, usually only seen in the far north. Also called the northern lights.

avalanche: a fall of a large mass of rock or snow down a mountainside.

basalt: a black, shiny volcanic rock.

biomass: the total mass of living things, both alive and recently living.

breed: to produce babies.

brittle: describes a solid that breaks when put under pressure. A blade of grass will bend, but a dry twig is brittle and will break.

caldera: a bowl-like depression at the top of a volcano. It forms when the magma chamber underneath is emptied and collapses.

Cascade Mountains: a range of volcanoes that runs from Canada through Washington and Oregon, ending in northern California.

Central Plateau: the relatively flat area in Alaska between the Brooks Range and the Alaska Range.

cetaceans: marine mammals that are nearly hairless with flippers and a flat notched tail, such as whales, dolphins, and porpoises.

Chinook wind: a dry, warm wind that blows on the eastern side of mountains in the Pacific Northwest.

cinder cone: a small, steep-sided volcano, built up by ash and smaller cinders.

climate: the average weather of an area over a long period of time.

Coast Ranges: ranges of mountains that run along the coastal areas of Alaska, Canada, Washington, Oregon, and northern California, including the Olympic Mountains.

Columbia Intermontane: the relatively flat area in Washington, Oregon, and Idaho between the Cascade and Rocky Mountains.

composite volcano: another name for a stratovolcano.

condense: when water vapor—a gas—changes back into liquid water.

continental United States: all of the states except for Alaska and Hawaii.

continental: relating to the earth's large land masses.

convergent boundary: where two plates come together.

core: the center of the earth, which is composed of the metals iron and nickel. The core has two parts—a solid inner core, and a liquid outer core.

crust: the thin, brittle, outer layer of the earth. Together with the upper mantle, it forms the lithosphere.

dam: a barrier across a river to hold back and control the water.

decompose: to break down, or rot, into simpler parts.

delaminate: when the lower part splits off.

divergent boundary: where two plates are moving in opposite directions, sometimes called a rift zone. New crust forms at rift zones from the magma pushing through the crust.

earthquake: a sudden movement in the outer layer of the earth that releases stress built up from the motion of the earth's plates.

ecosystem: a community of plants and animals living in the same area and relying on each other to survive.

eelgrass: a marine plant with long narrow leaves that grows in estuaries. Eelgrass supports a diverse habitat.

elevation: a measurement of height above sea level.

Pink Salmon

113

epicenter: the point on the earth's surface that is directly above the location of an earthquake.

epiphyte: a plant that lives on another plant. It gets its food and moisture directly from the air.

erosion: when a surface is worn away by wind or water.

estuary: a protected area where saltwater and freshwater mix together.

evaporate: when a liquid turns into a vapor or gas.

extinction: when a group of plants or animals dies out and there are no more left in the world.

fault: a crack in the outer layer of the earth where the rocks have moved past one another.

fine-grained: rock that has mineral grains that are too small to see.

fish ladder: a channel built around a dam that gradually rises from the water level below the dam to the water level above it.

fjord: a narrow, deep inlet of the sea with steep slopes on both sides.

flood basalt: a giant flow or a series of very large flows of lava that form basalt rocks.

Sockeye Salmon

fold and thrust belt: mountains that formed by one tectonic plate subducting under another and causing rocks farther inland to fold and be thrust over other rocks.

food web: a complex set of feeding relationships between plants and animals.

fossils: the remains or traces of ancient plants and animals.

fungi: a division of organisms including yeasts, molds, and mushrooms.

generate: to produce energy.

geography: the study of the earth and its features, especially the shape of the land, and the effect of human activity on the earth.

geologists: scientists who study the earth and its movements.

geology: the scientific study of the history and physical nature of the earth.

glacial lake: a lake that has been formed by a melted glacier.

glacier: a body of ice that slowly moves downhill due to gravity.

gorge: a deep, narrow passage.

habitat: the natural area where an animal, plant, or other organism lives.

hotspot: an area that can be found in the middle of a plate, where hot magma rises to the surface.

hydroelectric: electricity generated from the energy of flowing water.

hydrosphere: the earth's water, including oceans, rivers, lakes, glaciers, and water vapor in the air.

Ice Age: a period of time when glaciers covered a large part of the earth's surface.

igneous rocks: rocks that form from cooling magma.

intermontane: area between mountains.

irrigate: to supply land with water, usually for crops.

jet stream: a high-speed flow of air high in the atmosphere that flows from west to east and often brings weather with it.

Juan de Fuca Plate: a small oceanic plate off the coast of Washington and Oregon. It is subducting beneath the North American Plate.

kelp: large seaweed, which is a form of algae.

lahar: a mudflow that forms from lava and ash mixing with melted snow and rain. It can wipe out everything in its path.

landslide: rock and earth sliding down a slope due to gravity.

latitude: the angle of a location from the equator. The latitude is 0 degrees at the equator and 90 degrees at the North and South Poles.

lava tube: a cave-like channel through which lava used to flow.

lava: magma that has risen to the surface of the earth.

lichens: organisms that are part fungi and part algae.

lithosphere: the rigid outer layer of the earth that includes the crust and the upper mantle.

livestock: animals raised for food or other products.

magma: partially melted rock below the surface of the earth.

mammals: a class of animals that includes humans. Mammals have backbones and nourish their young with milk.

mantle: the middle layer of the earth. The upper mantle, together with the crust, forms the lithosphere.

marine: found in the ocean.

meandering river: a river that has large curves, or meanders. Meandering rivers generally occur on relatively flat plains.

Mediterranean climate: a climate that has moist, mild winters and warm, dry summers. This climate is named after the weather experienced by the land surrounding the Mediterranean Sea.

metamorphic rocks: rocks that have been transformed by heat or pressure or both into new rocks, while staying solid.

microscopic: so tiny that you need a microscope to see them.

midnight sun: when the sun stays above the horizon for 24 hours or more. This can occur only in latitudes above 60 degrees.

migrate: to move to another environment.

mycelium: the body of a fungus that is composed of many branching, threadlike filaments.

North American Plate: the plate that includes North America (continental crust) and the western half of the Atlantic Ocean (oceanic crust).

nurse log: a fallen, decomposing tree that provides shelter, moisture, and nutrients for insects and plants, especially young tree seedlings.

nutrients: the substances in food and soil that keep animals and plants healthy and growing.

obsidian: dark volcanic glass formed when lava cools so fast it can't form crystals.

oceanic: in or from the ocean.

organism: a living thing, such as a plant or animal.

Pangaea: a huge supercontinent that existed about 300 million years ago.

permafrost: the ground underneath the top layer of soil that is permanently frozen.

photosynthesis: the process where plants use sunlight and water to make their own food.

phytoplankton: microscopic plants that drift on the current.

pinnipeds: marine mammals that are fin-footed and include walruses, seals, and sea lions.

plate tectonics: the theory that describes how plates move across the earth and interact with each other to produce earthquakes, volcanoes, and mountains.

plateau: a relatively level, or flat area.

plates: huge, moving, interconnected slabs of lithosphere.

plume of magma: a large area of magma that rises to the surface from deep in the mantle. It has an upside-down teardrop shape.

polar night: when the sun stays below the horizon for 24 hours or more. This occurs only in latitudes above 60 degrees.

portage: to carry boats by land around a waterfall or other impassable part of a river.

precipitation: rain, snow, or any other form of water that falls to Earth.

predator: an animal that eats other animals.

pumice: a light rock full of air spaces, formed from solidified lava.

rain shadow: an area that is dry because it is on the side of a mountain away from the wind.

renewable resource: any natural resource that isn't used up, that can be replaced.

Richter scale: the scale for measuring the strength of an earthquake.

rifting: when the lithosphere splits apart.

ripple marks: parallel ridges formed from flowing water or air.

Rocky Mountains: a mountain range extending from New Mexico into Canada. The northern Rocky Mountains form the eastern boundary of the Pacific Northwest in Idaho and western Montana.

Rodinia: a huge supercontinent that existed about 1 billion years ago, containing all the land on Earth.

sanctuary: a place where wildlife is protected.

scabland: an area with deep, dry channels and rough, gouged rocks.

sedimentary rocks: rocks formed from the compression of sediments, the remains of plants or animals, or from the evaporation of seawater.

sediments: loose rock particles such as sand or clay.

shield volcano: a broad volcano formed from the flow of runny, non-explosive lava.

Snake River Plain: a boomerang-shaped area in southern Idaho that is relatively flat and contains basalt rocks.

sound: a long ocean inlet.

species: a group of plants or animals that are related and look like each other.

stratovolcano: a classic cone-shaped volcano with alternating layers of runny lava flows and more explosive volcanic deposits.

stromatolites: fossils of blue-green algae that lived in warm, shallow seas. Some are over 1½ billion years old.

subduction: when one tectonic plate slides underneath another tectonic plate.

subsistence: resources for survival.

swim bladder: an air-filled sac that many fish have to help them stay afloat.

tectonic: relating to forces that produce movement and changes in the earth's crust.

temperate rainforest: a forest in the temperate zone, halfway between the equator and the poles, that receives high rainfall.

thrusting: when rocks are pushed up and over another set of rocks.

transform boundary: where two plates slide against each other.

tributary: a stream or river that flows into a larger river.

tsunami: a series of giant waves caused by earthquakes, explosions, meteors, or landslides.

tundra: a plain in the far north where the soil below the surface is permanently frozen.

upwelling: when colder, denser, nutrient-rich water rises to the ocean's surface because the surface water has been diverted by wind.

vent: an opening in the earth's crust where molten lava and volcanic gases escape. Also called a fissure.

viscous: how thick and fluid a substance is. Honey is very viscous, while water is not.

volcanic dome: a volcano formed by thick lava oozing out. The lava is too thick to travel far and builds up into a dome.

volcano: a vent in the earth's surface through which magma, ash, and gases erupt.

watershed: the land area that drains into a river or stream.

wavelength: the distance from crest to crest in a series of waves.

wetlands: an area where the land is soaked with water. Wetlands are often important habitats for fish, plants, and wildlife.

Gray Wolves

BOOKS

Anderson; Alan; Gwen Diehn, and Terry Krautwurst. *Geology Crafts for Kids: 50 Nifty Projects to Explore the Marvels of Planet Earth.* New York: Sterling, 1998.

Blobaum, Cindy and Michael Kline. *Geology Rocks!: 50 Hands-On Activities to Explore the Earth.* Vermont: Williamson Publishing Company, 1999.

Farndon, John. *How the Earth Works.* New York: Dorling Kindersley Publishers Ltd, 1999.

Kent, Dcborah, *Oregon (America the Beautiful).* New York: Children's Press, 2008.

Mass, Cliff. *The Weather of the Pacific Northwest.* University of Washington Press, 2008.

Monterrey Bay Aquarium. *Sea Searcher's Handbook: Activities from the Monterrey Bay Aquarium.* Colorado: Roberts Rinehart Publishers, 1996.

Orr, Tamra. *Alaska (America the Beautiful).* New York: Children's Press, 2008.

Stefoff, Rebecca. *Washington (Celebrate the States).* New York: Marshall Cavendish, 2008.

Steffof, Rebecca. *Idaho (Celebrate the States).* New York: Marshall Cavendish, 2008.

Tagliaferro, Linda. *Explore the Tundra.* Capstone Press, 2008.

WEB SITES

- **http://www.maps.google.com** Satellite view of Pacific Northwest and Pacific Ocean. Click on the Satellite tab and scroll to wherever you want to look. You can zoom in or out. Be sure to check out the Pacific Ocean and Alaska.

- **http://www.nps.gov/** National Park Service main website. Click on links to find specific national parks and monuments.

- **http://emvc.geol.ucsb.edu/** Animations of plate tectonic history by the University of California Santa Barbara. Click on the Downloads tab, then the Regional Plate Tectonics and Geologic Histories link, then the download button under N.E. Pacific and W. North America Plate History, 38 Ma to Present (you can view other animations as well).

- **http://mineralsciences.si.edu/tdpmap/** World Interactive Map of Volcanoes, Earthquakes, Impact Craters, and Plate Tectonics, by Smithsonian, USGS, and US Naval Research Laboratory.

- **http://earthquake.usgs.gov/earthquakes/** Earthquakes in all states. Click on link on the left called "Earthquake Lists & Maps, then click on link "By State" to view information about a particular state. There are lots of other links with interesting information.

- **http://earthquake.usgs.gov/learn/kids/** U.S. Geological Survey Earthquakes for Kids site.

- **http://www.pbs.org/wnet/savageearth/** Volcanoes, earthquakes, tsunamis by PBS.

- **http://www.avo.alaska.edu/** Alaska Volcano Observatory, with interactive maps and webcams, and other information. There is also a link to the Cascades volcanoes.

- **http://www.nationalatlas.gov/dynamic/dyn_vol-ak.html** Dynamic map of volcanoes in Alaska. There are also links for the Cascades.

- **http://www.fs.fed.us/gpnf/volcanocams/msh/** Mount St. Helens VolcanoCam by the US Forest Service, with links to other real-time volcano cams.

- **http://www.fsvisimages.com/** Real-time images and air quality for various sites in the US Forest Service, including Columbia River Gorge and Mt. Hood.

- **http://water.usgs.gov/** Water Resources in the US by the USGS.

- **http://www.sanctuarysimon.org/monterey/** Monterrey Bay Aquarium, information on kelp forests, estuaries, rocky shores, and more.

- **http://www.nwr.noaa.gov** National Oceanic and Atmospheric Administration (NOAA) Northwest Regional Office, with information on marine mammals, salmon, hydroelectric power.

- **http://www.yukonenergy.ca** The Whitehorse Dam on the Yukon River and how hydroelectric plants work. Click on the link for Powerful Facts About Electricity.

- **http://www.osv.org/explore_learn/waterpower/** How waterwheels work and have been used in the past.

- **http://rainforests.pwnet.org/** America's Rain Forests by the US Forest Service.

INDEX

Chum Salmon